THE BASICS OF DATA LITERACY

HELPING YOUR STUDENTS *(AND YOU!)* MAKE SENSE OF DATA

NSTApress
National Science Teachers Association

THE BASICS OF DATA LITERACY

HELPING YOUR STUDENTS *(AND YOU!)* MAKE SENSE OF DATA

MICHAEL BOWEN
ANTHONY BARTLEY

National Science Teachers Association

Arlington, Virginia

National Science Teachers Association

Claire Reinburg, Director
Wendy Rubin, Managing Editor
Andrew Cooke, Senior Editor
Amanda O'Brien, Associate Editor
Amy America, Book Acquisitions Coordinator

ART AND DESIGN
Will Thomas Jr., Director
Rashad Muhammad, Graphic Designer

PRINTING AND PRODUCTION
Catherine Lorrain, Director

NATIONAL SCIENCE TEACHERS ASSOCIATION
David L. Evans, Executive Director
David Beacom, Publisher

1840 Wilson Blvd., Arlington, VA 22201
www.nsta.org/store
For customer service inquiries, please call 800-277-5300.

FSC
www.fsc.org
MIX
Paper from
responsible sources
FSC® C011935

NSTA is committed to publishing material that promotes the best in inquiry-based science education. However, conditions of actual use may vary, and the safety procedures and practices described in this book are intended to serve only as a guide. Additional precautionary measures may be required. NSTA and the authors do not warrant or represent that the procedures and practices in this book meet any safety code or standard of federal, state, or local regulations. NSTA and the authors disclaim any liability for personal injury or damage to property arising out of or relating to the use of this book, including any of the recommendations, instructions, or materials contained therein.

PERMISSIONS
Book purchasers may photocopy, print, or e-mail up to five copies of an NSTA book chapter for personal use only; this does not include display or promotional use. Elementary, middle, and high school teachers may reproduce forms, sample documents, and single NSTA book chapters needed for classroom or noncommercial, professional-development use only. E-book buyers may download files to multiple personal devices but are prohibited from posting the files to third-party servers or websites, or from passing files to non-buyers. For additional permission to photocopy or use material electronically from this NSTA Press book, please contact the Copyright Clearance Center (CCC) (*www.copyright.com*; 978-750-8400). Please access *www.nsta.org/permissions* for further information about NSTA's rights and permissions policies.

LIBRARY OF CONGRESS CATALOGING-IN-PUBLICATION DATA
Bowen, Michael, 1962-
  The basics of data literacy : helping your students (and you!) make better sense of data / Michael Bowen, Anthony Bartley.
    pages cm
  Includes bibliographical references and index.
  ISBN 978-1-938946-03-5 -- ISBN 978-1-938946-76-9 (e-book) 1. Science--Study and teaching. 2. Mathematics--Study and teaching. 3. Information literacy--Study and teaching. 4. Graphic methods. 5. Science--Tables. 6. Mathematics--Tables. I. Bartley, Anthony, 1950- II. Title.
  Q181.B7216 2013
  001.4071--dc23
                            2013028904

Cataloging-in-Publication Data for the e-book are available from the Library of Congress.

CONTENTS

ACKNOWLEDGMENTS

The idea for this book started developing 16 years ago when I was interviewing preservice teachers and other science program graduates about their interpretations of graphs as part of my PhD research. As I explored those issues further as a science methods instructor, I began creating resources and activities on this topic with my friend and colleague Tony Bartley. We subsequently produced a workshop that we have presented many, many times at NSTA conferences over the last decade. At those workshops, we gained more insights into the data literacy issues confronting teachers, in part from the many comments we collected from participants about resources they could use when doing investigations with their own students. The content and approach used in this book arose from those observations. At those meetings and others, Tony and I sat and hashed out the various activities, use of language, and explanations offered here.

My own interests in data and representations of it began during my undergraduate studies in 1982 when I took a research methods course with Hank Davis in the psychology department at the University of Guelph. The seed that Hank planted at that time in his long and productive career may be one that took the longest to flower, but I am glad that his efforts with me in that most interesting (and somewhat bizarre) class 30 years ago have borne such fruit. Thanks Hank. Then, my MS supervisor, John Sprague, pushed me into doing multidimensional modeling as part of my research in behavioral toxicology, and I was fortunate that software tools for the newly developed personal computers allowed me to play with graphical representations of data in his laboratory in ways that hadn't been possible even a few years earlier. That work was influential during my PhD research in science education because it gave me insights into how individuals gain competency in working with data. John Haysom, my science methods instructor (and now author of numerous NSTA Press books), further pushed me to figure out ways to develop children's interest in science investigations and, additionally, how to make abstract relationships more "real" to them by developing hands-on activities to help students experientially understand those relationships. Finally, my main academic influence has been Wolff-Michael Roth at the University of Victoria. My PhD work with him helped cast light (for me and others) on the role of graphical and tabular representations in science and how individuals at various educational levels gain understandings of (abstract) science concepts from those. He continues to push boundaries in these areas, and I admire his tenacity at teasing out the details of how understanding of science evolves. His academic achievements and his friendship have tremendously impacted my work on this project.

Finally, I would like to thank the many teachers and students who—through support, comments, advice, suggestions, and participation in hands-on activities with us—have helped generate this book.

It is my, and our, profound hope that you find this book useful for developing your students', and your own, understandings of how to work with data.

Mike Bowen
Halifax, Nova Scotia

ACKNOWLEDGMENTS

My journey in science education started in Liverpool (England!) many years ago when I completed a postgraduate certificate in Education at Saint Katherine's College of Education (now Liverpool Hope University). It was there I realized that most students I would meet in schools had very different views about their own education and where science fit in. I became a physics and chemistry teacher, first in Staffordshire, then West London, and finally in Kent; by extension, I also became a teacher of mathematics because we worked with data and problem sets.

Many of the people I worked with in England have now retired, but I remember both their mentorship and collegiality: Geoff Morris of the Ounsdale School (Wombourne), Hamish Miller of Christ's School (Richmond-upon-Thames), and Rick Armstrong of the Eden Valley School (Edenbridge) all deserve a mention, and thanks.

I moved to Canada in 1985 and taught in Victoria, British Columbia, from 1986 to 1989. In 1989 the University of British Columbia beckoned me for a PhD; it was here that I was lucky enough to work with Gaelen Erickson, Bob Carlisle, Jim Gaskell, and Dave Bateson as the home faculty members; Peter Fensham, Rosalind Driver, Cam McRobbie, and Ruth Stavy were notable visitors; and Tony Clarke and René Fountain were magnificent in their support as they too completed the doctoral journey.

I'm now approaching my 20th year at Lakehead University in Thunder Bay, Ontario. Mike was here for 5 of these years, and we have an enduring friendship through a broad range of collaborations in science education and other overlapping interests. My colleague now and for the last 8 years at Lakehead has been Wayne Melville, whose support for open inquiry has been consistent and strong; it helps us both that we have one of the strongest schools on the continent, Sir Winston Churchill Collegiate and Vocational Institute, just a few miles away. My appreciation as a university-based educator for the school-based support from the Churchill science department in learning science through inquiry, and its chair Doug Jones, cannot be overstated.

I have enjoyed this writing project and have learned a lot as Mike and I worked through our approaches over the last few years. I hope that this book and its ideas work for you and your students.

A. W. Bartley

A. W. Bartley
Thunder Bay, Ontario

FOREWORD

If you are a scientist or a science student, data literacy matters because it helps you make sense of information you've collected in lab investigations. But most students aren't going to be scientists, so why should developing data literacy be important? Isn't it enough to get them to know science concepts, remember facts and patterns, and draw graphs on tests? Where else would they encounter scientific data other than in a laboratory?

Although it may not seem like it, we are surrounded by data. When you open the newspaper and see a graph or a table as part of an article, what you're looking at is data. When you listen to news on the television or radio, what you're hearing are conclusions drawn from data someone else has collected. And they've collected that data to understand something, argue a position, make a point, or persuade the listeners to adopt a particular view. Some of these arguments are better than others because the data has been collected, analyzed, or summarized more effectively. This book is about understanding what good data and data analysis is so that you can make stronger arguments and better evaluate the arguments of others. It's important to realize that everyone has an agenda of some sort, and being more data literate helps you understand if others are making a fair argument.

Part of being able to take a more informed (some might say skeptical) view of data is being literate in how data are manipulated and subsequently presented: how they are collected, made into tables, and shown in pictures or graphs. Once you know how to do this the right way, such as you might learn in a science classroom, you can start asking if someone else is doing it in a way that is fair, or if they are distorting the data for their own purposes.

Data literacy is important for your students even if they aren't going to be scientists because data are used to argue and persuade people to, among other things, vote for political agendas, support specific types of spending within organizations, sell life insurance, or lease a car. An improved understanding of data practices means that better questions can be asked in all of these situations.

Even in everyday life, data collection can be important. Bakers often keep diaries when they're learning how to bake a new type of biscuit. Gardeners keep a log about the growth of their gardens, and birdwatchers keep track of where and when they see what types of birds and what the weather conditions were. Drivers keep track of vehicle mileage , and homeowners keep track of their electrical bill month to month. This is all real-life data. We could go on with examples like this forever, but now you can probably think of some data that you keep track of.

The point is, data literacy is an important skill to develop in students, and science classrooms are a good place to do that because data collection and interpretation are part of the science curriculum in most jurisdictions. Almost every teacher has faced the challenge of helping students make sense of some data set; many times, that teacher has sat there, scratched his or her head, and wondered how to help the students make sense of the data they collected. In science, there are some fundamental concepts that help scientists make sense of data, particularly the messy data found in the real world, and yet these fundamentals are infrequently taught in undergraduate science courses. Teachers who have their students do inquiry lab investigations can face data analysis challenges, even in a middle school science class, that exceed what they learned in their college science courses.

Learning about how to analyze and make better sense of data also helps you learn the best way to collect data. And learning how to collect, summarize, and analyze data is a very important science skill, central to the newly released *Next Generation Science Standards* (*NGSS*).

Lab investigations used to be pretty simple and straightforward (i.e., "cookbook labs"): The teacher provided a clear set of instructions; the students all engaged in the same activity, followed the same procedure, and were marked on getting the same "correct" answer. Then inquiry investigations came along, and classroom investigations got a lot more difficult. Many of us teachers didn't have a background sufficient for helping our students do those types of inquiry investigation activities.

The contrast between the two different types of lab activities could not be starker (Table F.1).

TABLE F.1

Comparing traditional laboratory activities with inquiry-based science investigations

	Traditional, structured, laboratory activities	Inquiry-based science investigations
Basis of learning	behaviorist	constructivist
Curricular goals	product-oriented (i.e., everyone gets the same answer)	process-oriented (with some product)
Role of student	following directions	problem solver/arguer
Student participation	passive/receptive	active
Student ownership of project	lower	higher
Student involvement	lower responsibility	higher responsibility
Role of teacher	director/transmitter	guide/facilitator

As every teacher understands, supporting students who are doing laboratory investigations of the student-directed and open-ended type (such as those in the Inquiry-Based Science column would usually be) is a considerable challenge and can require a lot more background knowledge than undergraduate teaching programs often provide. Some teacher preparation programs have specific courses that deal with doing inquiry, thus allowing student teachers to learn the basics of data literacy, but many do not.

What we (the authors) realized some years ago is that the challenge in encouraging teachers to do inquiry investigations exists in part because of aspects of data collection, analysis, synthesis, and presentation that teachers of science often just do not know. Nor, as far as we could tell, are there good resources geared toward helping them learn the material in a way that would be useful for their students. To address this, we developed and have presented a workshop on data literacy at the national NSTA conferences for the last several years. The workshop has been quite popular, but what we have since realized is that a more comprehensive resource, building on the workshop, would be useful for science teachers. This book grew out of that realization. We've tried to write it so that it is pretty approachable by using a minimum of technical language. And we've tried to use examples that relate to classrooms and the types of data collection activities that teachers have students do. We hope you find it useful in helping your classes become more data literate.

WHO IS THIS BOOK FOR?

- Teachers who need to read government and school board documents that present data in tables or graphs will find most chapters useful to read over to help their understanding of those documents.

- Teachers of lower elementary grades (whenever they start students interpreting bar charts or histograms) will find the early chapters useful.

- Middle school teachers will find the first eight chapters helpful.

- High school teachers will benefit from reading the entire book, and in particular the later chapters if they have advanced students who need to be challenged with more complex work.

- Individuals working on a graduate degree that involves data collection will find this a good introduction to any research methods course they might need to take.

The appendixes provide laboratory investigation activities (Appendixes I and II) to help you teach these data representation and analysis concepts to your students at various grade levels. In addition, there are appendixes to help you evaluate the laboratory activities your students have handed in (Appendixes III and IV) as well as a collection of data analysis worksheets with examples of quantitative data analysis (Appendixes VIII and IX) that can be used by upper-level students to help them conduct more detailed analyses of data they've collected in lab investigations.

CONNECTIONS TO THE *FRAMEWORK* AND THE STANDARDS

Our work in writing this book took place at the same time as the development of the *NGSS* in the United States. The guiding document for the *NGSS*—*A Framework for K–12 Science Education: Practices, Crosscutting Concepts, and Core Ideas* (*Framework*; NRC 2012)—sets out eight scientific and engineering practices, of which Analyzing and Interpreting Data is the fourth on the list. The *Framework* identifies the grade 12 goals for analyzing and interpreting data as follows:

- Analyze data systematically, either to look for salient patterns or to test whether data are consistent with an initial hypothesis.

- Recognize when data are in conflict with expectations and consider what revisions in the initial model are needed.

- Use spreadsheets, databases, tables, charts, graphs, statistics, mathematics, and information and computer technology to collate, summarize, and display data and to explore relationships between variables, especially those representing input and output.

- Evaluate the strength of a conclusion that can be inferred from any data set, using appropriate grade-level mathematical and statistical techniques.

- Recognize patterns in data that suggest relationships worth investigating further. Distinguish between causal and correlational relationships.

- Collect data from physical models and analyze the performance of a design under a range of conditions. (NRC 2012, pp. 62–63)

PROGRESSIONS IN THE *FRAMEWORK*

This is a quick look at the Analyzing and Interpreting Data progressions found in the *Framework* document.

In elementary classes, we would see students

- make a start at recording and sharing observations; and

- engage in scientific inquiry and begin collecting categorical or numerical data for presentation in forms that facilitate interpretation, such as tables and graphs.

In middle school, students would learn the use and justification of some of the standard techniques for displaying, analyzing, and interpreting data, including

- different types of graphs;
- the identification of outliers in the data set; and
- averaging to reduce the effects of measurement error.

In high school, as the complexity of investigations increases, we see a broadening of the techniques for the display and analysis of the data. Examination of the relationships between two variables sees students produce *x-y* scatterplots or crosstabulations.

THE *NGSS*

The table below is taken from the *NGSS* (p. 9, Appendix F; NGSS Lead States 2013); it clearly shows the significance of data literacy and the related progressions that have been developed at the state standard level (Figure F.1).

FIGURE F.1

Progression of the practice of analyzing data in the *NGSS*

Grades K-2	Grades 3-5	Grades 6-8	Grades 9-12
Analyzing data in K–2 builds on prior experiences and progresses to collecting, recording, and sharing observations. • Record information (observations, thoughts, and ideas). • Use and share pictures, drawings, and/or writings of observations. • Use observations (firsthand or from media) to describe patterns and/or relationships in the natural and designed world(s) in order to answer scientific questions and solve problems. • Compare predictions (based on prior experiences) to what occurred (observable events). • Analyze data from tests of an object or tool to determine if it works as intended.	Analyzing data in 3–5 builds on K–2 experiences and progresses to introducing quantitative approaches to collecting data and conducting multiple trials of qualitative observations. When possible and feasible, digital tools should be used. • Represent data in tables and/or various graphical displays (bar graphs, pictographs and/or pie charts) to reveal patterns that indicate relationships. • Analyze and interpret data to make sense of phenomena, using logical reasoning, mathematics, and/or computation. • Compare and contrast data collected by different groups in order to discuss similarities and differences in their findings. • Analyze data to refine a problem statement or the design of a proposed object, tool, or process. • Use data to evaluate and refine design solutions.	Analyzing data in 6–8 builds on K–5 experiences and progresses to extending quantitative analysis to investigations, distinguishing between correlation and causation, and basic statistical techniques of data and error analysis. • Construct, analyze, and/or interpret graphical displays of data and/or large data sets to identify linear and nonlinear relationships. • Use graphical displays (e.g., maps, charts, graphs, and/or tables) of large data sets to identify temporal and spatial relationships. • Distinguish between causal and correlational relationships in data. • Analyze and interpret data to provide evidence for phenomena. • Apply concepts of statistics and probability (including mean, median, mode, and variability) to analyze and characterize data, using digital tools when feasible. • Consider limitations of data analysis (e.g., measurement error), and/or seek to improve precision and accuracy of data with better technological tools and methods (e.g., multiple trials). • Analyze and interpret data to determine similarities and differences in findings. • Analyze data to define an optimal operational range for a proposed object, tool, process or system that best meets criteria for success.	Analyzing data in 9–12 builds on K–8 experiences and progresses to introducing more detailed statistical analysis, the comparison of data sets for consistency, and the use of models to generate and analyze data. • Analyze data using tools, technologies, and/or models (e.g., computational, mathematical) in order to make valid and reliable scientific claims or determine an optimal design solution. • Apply concepts of statistics and probability (including determining function fits to data, slope, intercept, and correlation coefficient for linear fits) to scientific and engineering questions and problems, using digital tools when feasible. • Consider limitations of data analysis (e.g., measurement error, sample selection) when analyzing and interpreting data. • Compare and contrast various types of data sets (e.g., self-generated, archival) to examine consistency of measurements and observations. • Evaluate the impact of new data on a working explanation and/or model of a proposed process or system. • Analyze data to identify design features or characteristics of the components of a proposed process or system to optimize it relative to criteria for success.

WHAT ABOUT MATH? WHERE DOES DATA LITERACY FIT IN THERE?

Two guiding documents connect math to data literacy. The *Principles and Standards for School Mathematics* (NCTM 2000) has a strand entitled Data Analysis and Probability and the *Common Core State Standards, Mathematics* (NGAC and CCSSO 2010) has Measurement and Data as well as Statistics and Probability.

USE OF DATA IN THE NCTM PRINCIPLES AND STANDARDS

The big ideas guiding the NCTM Principles and Standards are that all students should be able to

- formulate questions that can be addressed with data and to collect, organize, and display relevant data to answer them;
- select and use appropriate statistical methods to analyze data;
- develop and evaluate inferences and predictions that are based on data; and
- understand and apply basic concepts of probability.

Looking at graphing, we see the following progression:

- K–2: Represent data using concrete objects, pictures, and graphs
- 3–5: Represent data using tables and graphs such as line plots, bar graphs, and line graphs
- 6–8: Select, create, and use appropriate graphical representations of data, including histograms, box plots, and scatterplots
- 9–12: Understand histograms, parallel box plots, and scatterplots and use them to display data

REFERENCES TO USE OF DATA IN THE *COMMON CORE STATE STANDARDS, MATHEMATICS*

The strand Measurement and Data runs from first to fifth grade, with Statistics and Probability running from sixth grade to high school. Let's look at the progression.

MEASUREMENT AND DATA

- Grade 1: Organize, represent, and interpret data with up to three categories
- Grade 2: Draw a picture graph and, in high school, a bar graph (with single-unit scale) to represent a data set with up to four categories
- Grade 3: Draw a scaled picture graph and a scaled bar graph to represent a data set with several categories
- Grade 4: Make a line plot to display a data set of measurements in fractions of a unit (½, ¼, ⅛)

- Grade 5: Use operations on fractions for this grade to solve problems involving information presented in line plots

STATISTICS AND PROBABILITY

- Grade 6: Recognize a statistical question as one that anticipates variability in the data related to the question and accounts for it in the answers
- Grade 7: Use measures of center and measures of variability for numerical data from random samples to draw informal comparative inferences about two populations
- Grade 8: (1) Construct and interpret scatter plots for bivariate measurement data to investigate patterns of association between two quantities
- Grade 8: (2) Know that straight lines are widely used to model relationships between two quantitative variables. For scatter plots that suggest a linear association, informally fit a straight line, and informally assess the model fit by judging the closeness of the data points to the line

INTERPRETING CATEGORICAL AND QUANTITATIVE DATA

Grades 9–12: High School

- Summarize, represent, and interpret data on a single count or measurement variable
- Summarize, represent, and interpret data on two categorical and quantitative variables
- Interpret linear models

The above information on science and math standards was obtained directly from the documents listed in the Reference section (and as such much of the text is a direct copy from those documents).

REFERENCES

National Council of Teachers of Mathematics (NCTM). 2000. *Principles and standards for school mathematics*. Reston, VA: National Council of Teachers of Mathematics.

National Governors Association Center for Best Practices and Council of Chief State School Officers (NGAC and CCSSO). 2010. *Common core state standards*. Washington, DC: NGAC and CCSSO.

National Research Council (NRC). 2012. *A framework for K–12 science education: Practices, crosscutting concepts, and core ideas*. Washington, DC: National Academies Press.

NGSS Lead States. 2013. *Next Generation Science Standards: For states, by states*. Washington, DC: National Academies Press. *www.nextgenscience.org/next-generation-science-standards*.

SECTION I
FUNDAMENTALS OF SHOWING, ANALYZING, AND DISCUSSING DATA

This section introduces how to show your data (such as in graphs and tables) and discusses the basics of data analysis (from a visual and conceptual perspective).

WHAT

Here we introduce the different types of data variables and the types of graphs that are usually used to represent them in science. These data types include the very simple sort that can be shown in bar graphs (or charts, sometimes called histograms), which students even in the low primary grades can use. The types of data shown in line graphs and scatterplots are often used in middle school grades (i.e., grades 5–8) and above.

For each of these three data types, there is a worked-through activity using very simple equipment (paper, Styrofoam, and plastic cups; marbles; and a 12" ruler with a groove) that you can use to teach your students about these concepts. We provide details within these activities about how to coach your students through the analysis of the data.

We also provide worked-through examples of how to interpret the data shown in the graphs and how to discuss that data using the types of language scientists would use. This will help your students both make sense of their own data *and* better understand the data and claims they read about elsewhere.

Here's the cool part of this section (at least for us): these activities involve no measuring or arithmetic. You can teach your students the fundamentals of graphing and data analysis as scientists would do it without students' issues with math confounding their understanding.

WHO

We have done NSTA conference workshops on these issues for years, and both high school science teachers and primary or elementary teachers have told us that the ideas are useful for their teaching of science and math. In our own experience, we have found the ideas useful for helping teach both incoming primary or elementary science teachers about science as well as in teaching our secondary science methods courses about how to think about data analysis. Yup … that's a pretty broad range, but data literacy is both *that* important and yet is taught *that* little in undergraduate classes.

HOW

At most grade levels now, students are expected to engage in some form of data collection activity. Often these involve open-ended sorts of questions for which students are to collect data and make arguments. In middle and upper grades, this may be done through inquiry activities at first and then in science fair projects. To help prepare students for those sorts of explorations, teachers can use the lessons modeled in Chapters 3–5 (see Appendix I for example assignments) and then have students do investigations such as those outlined in Appendix II to help reinforce the ideas about analyzing evidence, drawing conclusions, and writing claims about their observations.

CHAPTER 1
INTRODUCTION: DATA AND SCIENCE

Data, whether quantitative (measurements, counts, and so on) or qualitative (color, movement, description of sound or smell, and so on), lies at the very heart of how scientists make sense of the world and construct and report patterns in it. Thus, an important part of science literacy is data literacy.

Being able to collect and use your own data to examine the world for patterns is an important skill for anyone to have, even if they're not a scientist. Whether it's learning to cook a steak perfectly by keeping a cooking diary or figuring out how to get the best mileage from your car by keeping a gasoline consumption and distance log, making structured observations and understanding the patterns in them uses the same data literacy tools that scientists use.

SCIENTISTS AND DATA

The claims and arguments made in science almost always extend from data that scientists have collected. Usually, though not always, that data involves counts, measurements, or some other quantitative determination. Scientists then analyze their data using tables, graphs, or statistical analyses—or all of these.

So why do scientists use graphs? Why don't they just look at the data tables? The answer to that has two parts that are sort of related. First, graphs often represent a summary of numbers so that you're not (usually, anyways) looking at as much information. Second, it can be difficult to see patterns in large sets of numbers but easier to see them in graphs. Basically, graphs make understanding the patterns of relationships between variables easier.

Science is ultimately about making *predictive models*. In other words, science is constructing regular patterns (using either a graph or a formula) and then using them to make predictions. If you think about the *x-y* graph that you learned to make in grade 7 or 8, that's a simple science model. For instance, a graph showing the relationship between the amount of water you drank due to thirst and how warm the room was is a simple *x-y* model. You could then use that graph to predict how much water you'd need to take with you to watch a baseball game at a park (Figure 1.1).

FIGURE 1.1

Simple *x-y* graph with labeled axes

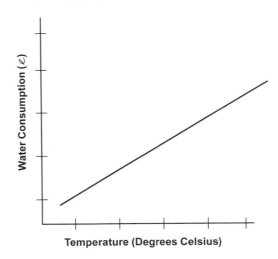

But science often makes models more complex than that. A more elaborate graph for the baseball game prediction could include an axis for humidity, which also influences the amount of water you need to drink (Figure 1.2, p. 4).

FIGURE 1.2

Three-axis *x-y-z* graph with labeled axes

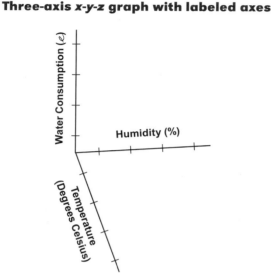

You can see that this could become quite complex very quickly. What if there was another variable such as the amount of shade? Frankly, our brains hurt even trying to think of how that graph would look.

Don't worry—this book isn't about dealing with data that intricate. We decided to focus instead on some basics that will help make you (and your students) comfortable with working simple relationships between variables to help give you a solid understanding of those.

So, how do scientists learn about using graphs properly to make sense of data?

Just as with many research practices, scientists often learn about graphing practices in informal ways. When scientists go to conferences, they see other scientists doing things with data that they hadn't thought of doing with their own, and they try out those approaches themselves later. It also helps that when scientists are in their home laboratory they work in heterogeneous (or mixed) communities with people from different backgrounds who can suggest new ways of working with the data.

Teachers and students don't often have those advantages. The communities they work in are quite stable, without much variety in experience. This can make doing a good job with data analysis more difficult because there are fewer suggestions about how to analyze the data. This book will provide you, the teacher, with some background to help you help your students do a better job of showing their data (in tables and graphs) and then draw better conclusions from it.

So, let's get started. First, we're going to discuss a few ways of thinking about data that often aren't emphasized in undergraduate science classes, but which we think will be helpful in better understanding data. Reading over this section will give you some background that is useful for understanding later chapters.

SCIENCE AND PROBABILITIES

Science is a probabilistic endeavor, meaning that it doesn't make absolute deterministic statements (i.e., this causes that); it makes statements of probability (i.e., this likely causes that, and we are very/pretty/sort of certain about that). This might seem a bit unusual because textbooks often present science in a very deterministic way, but that's not how scientists usually write about their findings, and more importantly, it's not how they understand what they read.

Sometimes when you read what scientists write, it appears quite deterministic. But scientists write for other scientists, and what we know from working with such researchers is that at the core of their writing is an implicit, unspoken understanding that the reader (most often a professional colleague) will make sense of what they write probabilistically, not as an absolute statement of truth. This practice is accepted as a given amongst scientists. But problems arise when others, especially non-scientists, read their work and interpret what they write from a different perspective—a deterministic perspective.

For example, school science textbooks are usually written using very deterministic language, so students take away from them the perspective that the facts presented are absolutes. But this is a misrepresentation of the writing and reading practices of scientists.

How often do we read in the newspaper that an issue needs to be studied more to get the answer about a science issue? How might thinking of science claims as deterministic affect this? If you think probabilistically about the knowledge you have, then "more research" is *always* needed, but if you think deterministically about science claims, then hearing that more research is needed suggests that not enough is known to make a strong claim about a relationship, and therefore there may not be any reason to act yet (global warming is a good example of this).

How can you, as a teacher, help your students develop an understanding of the probabilistic nature of science claims? In what ways can students work with graphs so that they start thinking about the probabilistic nature of science?

In examining science textbooks, it is clear that the graphs often present data very deterministically. And, interestingly, most science teaching reinforces that deterministic perspective. For instance, many traditional science laboratory activities expect students to come up with a *specific* answer, and students are marked according to how close they are to that answer. Getting a specific answer—requiring a specific answer—reinforces a deterministic perspective of science.

How can we break away from this deterministic way of looking at science and help students better understand the probabilistic nature of science?

One approach is to get students to work with "messier" data.

THE "MESS" OF REAL-WORLD DATA

School data, the types that come from many traditional school investigation activities, are often quite sanitized. In other words, the relationship between the variables is often unambiguous, and if you drew a graph of the data, the pattern you saw in the graph would be clear; school-based investigations are often designed to produce a nice and clean, straight-line relationship between variables without any data deviating from the line of best fit. On top of that, textbooks often show graphs that have clear and unambiguous patterns in the relationships between variables. However, in contrast with what is shown in textbooks or the expected outcomes of traditional science classroom laboratory investigations, most relationships in the real world (the world in which we actually experience friction, among other things) are not that clear. There are often other intervening variables that we cannot actually control. Real-world data relationships are often pretty messy, with lots of variation in them so that the data points are widely scattered around the mean or the line of best fit.

So, why would teaching students about these unambiguous relationships found in textbooks or traditional lab activities be a problem? Because it affects students' understanding of more ambiguous relationships—the types of relationships found in real-world data. As a case in point, research suggests that if relationships are not absolutely clear (i.e., in "science talk" that they have a very high r-squared[1]), many students will claim that no relationship exists when examining a data set.[2] However, a scientist looking at the same data set would claim that a relationship *did* exist, even if it wasn't perfect, because one variable actually did correspond to another to some degree. What this means is that the clean relationships of textbooks and traditional laboratory activities implicitly teach students that relationships between variables must be perfect, without variation, to make any claims about a relationship existing. This does not reflect the actual practices of science.

This suggests that it is actually very important to have students make sense of relationships that are less than perfect (such as those often reported in open-inquiry investigations) because those relationships better reflect ones that exist in real-world data and will better develop students' science literacy skills.

OPEN-INQUIRY LABORATORY ACTIVITIES

Open-inquiry science investigations allow students to have some freedom in design of the investigation, particularly in cases in which the outcome is unknown and must be argued for. There is a scaled taxonomy of inquiry (or investigation) studies that relate to resources, outcomes, and guidance. This taxonomy is generally as follows:

Confirmatory (or "cookbook" labs; expected outcomes) → structured investigations → guided investigations → open inquiry.

One way of understanding this is to look at the characteristics of open-inquiry investigations. Open inquiry student work is often characterized by investigating a problem that

- is ill-defined (allowing room for modification of the project as students proceed);

- allows students to experience uncertainties and ambiguities when drawing conclusions, as is typically found in professional science (i.e., hedging language, discussed in Chapter 7);

- starts at the current knowledge state of the students in each project and is used to locate the conceptual foundations of an acceptable project (i.e., start where they are);

- allows material and discursive practices and resources to be shared and developed within communities of learners (i.e., students talk to each other about their project work both during and after an inquiry activity); and

- offers the opportunity for newcomers to the community (often the students) to draw on the expertise of others (students, teaching assistants, teachers, other adults, professors) or on any other suitable resource that could enhance their learning and engagement in their investigation. (i.e., a mixed experience community is important). (Roth and Bowen 1995).

Another way of examining student activities is by using a system designed by Pinchas

---

1. We'll explain and illustrate ideas and terms similar to this in Chapter 8.

2. If you look at the diagram in Chapter 5, Figure 5.9, students often only accept that a relationship exists if the relationship between variables looks like (A), even though definitely (B) and probably (C) would likely be statistically acceptable—although both are weaker relationships with less predictive ability than (A).

Tamir (1991; which, you'll note, relates to the descriptions at Level 3; Table 1.1).

TABLE 1.1

Levels of science inquiry

Level of inquiry	Problems	Procedures	Conclusions
0	given	given	given
1	given	given	open
2	given	open	open
3	open	open	open

In their research work, scientists generally work at Level 3 (although graduate students are often working at a problem that has been somewhat defined for them).

Teachers can set their students up for working at higher level activities through the types of questions they ask. For one lesson, a teacher could find a plot of grass outside the school and ask students to calculate an estimate of the number of blades of grass in the area, taking into account patchiness (density differences) if necessary. This type of activity can be tied into many biological concepts and can be made more and more detailed for older and older students, but even grade 8 students can calculate these estimates. It is an authentic sort of open-inquiry investigation because there *is* a finite amount of grass there, but no one really knows what that amount is. Students must argue for what they believe to be correct. And arguing, as science teachers know, is a key science skill.

From our perspective, it is important to note two things if you want to use Tamir's Levels of Science Inquiry scale to plan activities for your students. First, students generally need to be scaffolded toward working at higher-level investigations. Second, "open" does not mean free reign to do anything one wants. Science is bounded by conventions and to be working like scientists students must be working within those conventions.

And, it is important to note, when using the table there are shades of gray in deciding how open an activity needs to be. Teachers can define part of an activity (such as counting blades of grass), which then has multiple problems embedded within it for the students to define. In our view, the blades of grass problem lies between Level 2 and Level 3 in the problem category.

OPEN INQUIRY AND HIGHER-ORDER THINKING SKILLS

One reason for moving toward engaging students in open-inquiry investigations is that they better reflect the types of studies done by scientists. On top of that, there are broader educational reasons: open-inquiry investigations are highly related to the types of activities that develop higher-order thinking skills. In her book *Education and Learning to Think* (1987), Lauren Resnick describes higher-order thinking as follows:

- nonalgorithmic, that is, the path of action is not fully specified in advance
- complex, with the total path not visible from any single vantage point
- often yielding multiple solutions, each with costs and benefits
- involving nuanced judgement and interpretation
- involving the application of multiple criteria, some of which may conflict

- often involving uncertainty because not everything that bears on the task is known
- involving self-regulation of the thinking process, rather than coaching at each step
- involving imposing meaning and finding structure in apparent disorder
- is effortful, with considerable mental work involved

The connections between higher-order thinking and open-inquiry investigation activities are reasonably obvious, and part of the reason for encouraging teachers to have students do open-inquiry investigations is that they help develop higher-order cognitive skills.

IT'S NOT JUST DIFFERENCES THAT MATTER WHEN DRAWING CONCLUSIONS IN SCIENCE

School science tends to focus on differences between means (or averages) or slopes in having students draw conclusions. This seems *similar* to what scientists do, but in reality it is an artifact of the types of data found in traditional school laboratory activities, which have very low variation in the data (as discussed in the previous section). What do we mean by this?

Simply put, the nonmessy relationships portrayed in textbooks and traditional lab activities (in which one correct answer is expected) mean that looking at *only* the means (or averages) makes sense in the data analysis because there is little or no variation of data points around those means. This then leads students to draw deterministic answers (and think about science that way) rather than developing probabilistic perspectives on science knowledge claims.

Let's look at an example of how students are usually taught to interpret data. In the bar graph below (Figure 1.4), we show data that comes from exposing two thermometers to sunlight in the classroom window for five minutes. In this study, one thermometer has the bulb covered in gray paint and the other has the bulb covered in white paint (Figure 1.3).

FIGURE 1.3

Sketch of classroom windows with pairs of thermometers on the counter

If we had groups of students do this activity, then one group's data might end up showing a graph like that in Figure 1.4.

FIGURE 1.4

Bar graph showing the difference in temperature between the gray thermometer and the white thermometer after five minutes in the Sun

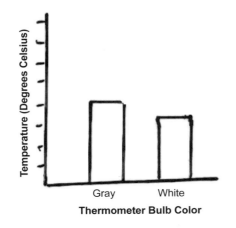

Thermometer Bulb Color

FIGURE 1.5

Bar graph showing some difference in temperatures between the gray thermometer and the white thermometer after five minutes in the Sun, averaged for the whole class

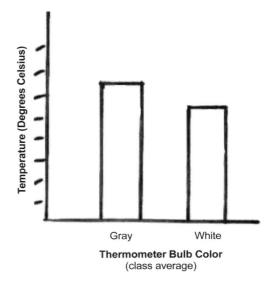

Thermometer Bulb Color
(class average)

It would not be unusual for the teacher to have each group draw conclusions from their own graph of the data. What might a student deduce from this graph? Many students might determine that the gray-painted thermometer bulb absorbed more energy from the Sun, and therefore the temperature went up more than it did with the white-coated thermometer bulb. It's not a big difference, but still, when we're dealing with absolutes, it's a difference. (You might want to think about this activity looking back at the Science and Probabilities section).

Of course, in science there are usually replicates of studies. So, what if we collected all the classroom data from each group (which is a type of replicate), calculated the arithmetic average, and then plotted it in a bar graph? Then the graph might look like Figure 1.5.

So, again, what might a student decide is happening from *this* graph? Despite the slightly different look to the bar heights, their answer might well be the same as the one arrived at from Figure 1.4. It's still not a big difference, but there is definitely a difference between the two averages.

So, is this how a scientist would draw conclusions from the data?

Surprisingly, no. Scientists *do* look at the averages and compare them, just as the students would, but there is *another* factor that is just as important to the scientists—the dispersion (or scatter) of the data around the averages. Unlike what is often taught in school science, scientists draw conclusions by examining the averages *and* the dispersion of the data around those averages (they often calculate this as a standard deviation).

Simply put, if the dispersions of the data for the two different means overlap a lot, then that affects the sort of conclusions that scientists draw. If the data overlap only a little, then scientists would make different determinations.

Let's take a look at an example using Figure 1.5. We're going to do something to Figure 1.5 that almost never gets done to bar graphs: we're going to plot the raw data from each group on it.[3] Imagine that the data varies between the groups quite a bit. Then the graph might look like Figure 1.6.

FIGURE 1.6

The graph from Figure 1.5 with raw data plotted above and below each mean (wide data spread)

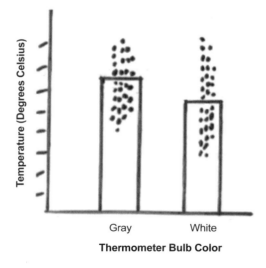

In this instance (Figure 1.6) because of how much the data varies around each of the averages (i.e., where the tops of the bars are),

a scientist might conclude that there's no real difference in temperature for the white- and gray-covered bulbs. That's because the data for each thermometer for the whole class (students did lots of replicates) overlapped quite a lot for each of the two thermometer bulb colors.

But what if the raw data looked like that in Figure 1.7, with a much narrower range of data scatter? What type of conclusions might be drawn by a scientist from this graph?

FIGURE 1.7

The graph from Figure 1.5 with raw data plotted above and below each mean (narrow data spread)

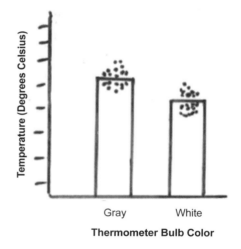

The lack of overlap of the data scatter in relation to the mean temperatures for each bulb color would suggest to a scientist that the means *are* different. The scientists could be "pretty darned sure" that the final temperatures were different and therefore that the color of the bulb *did* make a difference in the amount of energy absorbed by the thermometer.

---

3. Here we are showing an analysis of this data graphically in Figures 1.6 and 1.7. For a statistical analysis of this same data, see Appendix VIII.

See? The amount of data scatter around the means in the bar graph can lead to different conclusions. The average temperatures for the gray and white bulb are the same as depicted in Figures 1.6 and 1.7, but the way in which the data are scattered around those means influences the type of conclusion that is drawn.

So, this relationship between the means and the scatter of your data is an important part of interpreting data and therefore an important part of developing students' data literacy. Schools don't usually teach this, but maybe they should.

Here's the thing: It's not all that difficult to teach kids to analyze data and talk about them using these ideas, particularly if the students get to play with data that are a bit messy. (Just so you know, by *messy* we mean data with variation in it, like that in Figure 1.5, in case the term messy is still confusing you a bit.)

Now we've covered some of the basics—how science is probabilistic, how real-world data are often messy, and how scientists draw conclusions from data—and that should help the next few chapters make a bit more sense.

REFERENCES

Resnick, L. 1987. *Education and learning to think*. Washington, DC: National Academies Press

Roth W. -M., and G. M. Bowen. 1995. Knowing and interacting: A study of culture, practice, and resources in grade 8 open-inquiry science classroom guided by a cognitive apprenticeship metaphor. *Cognition and Instruction* 13 (1): 73–128.

Tamir, P. 1991. Practical work in school science: An analysis of current practice. In *Practical Science*, ed. B. Woolnough, 13–20. Milton Keynes, UK: Open University Press.

CHAPTER 2
AN INTRODUCTION TO UNDERSTANDING TYPES OF VARIABLES AND DATA

In order to understand how to enter your data into tables, it's important you grasp a basic issue about the relationship between types of independent variables and the kinds of graphs used to show them. So, what we're going to do first is briefly discuss the types of data and the differences between them. (Each type subsequently has its own chapter with more details.)

A TYPOGRAPHY OF DATA VARIABLES

Generally, there are three different categories of independent variables,[1] or independent variable types. Professional science infrequently uses the first, sometimes uses the second, and often uses the third (Table 2.1).

Nominal data are data collected from two unrelated independent variables. For instance, you could measure the running speed of dogs and cats and compare the two averages. Or you could measure the lengths of carrots grown in two different types of soil. However, in science this isn't considered a very "strong" type of variable because (1) usually all it can do is show the differences between the two categories, and (2) you usually cannot predict what would happen with a third category. For example, just because you know the running

TABLE 2.1

Types of independent variables

Type	Description	Example
Nominal	category data	dogs and cats, types of fruit, male and female
Ordinal	ordered category	size of coffee cups, shirt sizes
Interval-ratio	measures or counts with a (potential) zero	length of your arm in centimeters, grams of sugar, number of salt packets

speeds of cats and dogs doesn't mean you can predict how fast rabbits are. Because of its limited ability for prediction, nominal-level data are thought of as a "lower order" data type. **In science, nominal data are usually depicted in a bar graph.**[2]

Ordinal data are collected from independent variables that are related to each other but not in a way that is measured. For instance, coffee cups come in sizes small, medium, large, and extra large. However, there isn't an arithmetic relationship between these sizes. A medium isn't half again as big as a small, a large isn't half again as big as a medium; or twice as big; or 15% as big. The data are considered ordinal because of the *relative* ordered relationship between the different categories. Nor does that relationship have to be on a size-related scale either. It could be "red, redder, reddest"

---

1. Independent variables are the variables that you're changing or comparing, dependent variables are what you are measuring in response to the change/comparison. Usually the independent variables go on the horizontal axis of a graph. In our work with students, we've often found it more effective to talk about cause (*x*-axis) and effect (*y*-axis) variables. Sometimes you can find studies with two correlational variables where one isn't causing the other (such as the relationship between arm length and leg length) but instead they're both affected by a third (unstudied) variable.

2. We are, of course, presenting generalities. Those variable types are also sometimes represented using other graph types, but we are discussing the type of graphical representation most normally associated with each variable type in science.

or "sorta smelly, smelly, smellier, smelliest"— just as long as there is an increasing order to things. Ordinal data variables are considered stronger (or higher order) than nominal data variables because you can do some simple sorts of predictions from them, but without a lot of precision. **In science, ordinal data are normally depicted in a line graph** (sometimes, although much less often, they are depicted in a bar graph).

Interval-ratio data are those independent variables for which there are direct measures (or counts) that are proportional against a consistent scale. For instance, the distance from 15 to 20 m is exactly the same as that from 30 to 35 m. Twenty freckles is exactly twice as many as 10 freckles. That seems quite straightforward doesn't it? Here's another way of thinking about these variables: 2 g of salt is twice as much as 1 g of salt, and 4 g of salt is twice as much as 2 g of salt. So, the ratios between the amounts are consistent, unlike in the ordinal variables for which we only know that a medium cup is bigger than a small cup, but not by how much (there's no ratio, or multiplier, there). Usually when there is a measure (or count) of something (e.g., temperature, length, frequency, speed) that involves units, you're dealing with an interval-ratio variable. Interval-ratio measurements are the most common form of variable used in science because they give the best opportunity to make predictions. Because of this strong predictive ability, interval-ratio data are considered to be a strong or higher-order type of data. **In science, interval-ratio data are normally depicted in a scatterplot graph,** and often a line of best fit (or a trend bar, which we'll argue might be better in a later chapter) is drawn through the main data pattern if possible.

WHY GRAPHING RAW DATA MATTERS

Okay, we sort of talked about this topic in Chapter 1, but we're going to do it again in this section because of how important we think it is[3]—and that is the importance of raw and messy data. Typically, in school science, students graph averages of data but then ignore the data dispersion information. As we mentioned before, this is probably because the clean relationships that are chosen for traditional school science activities normally have little or no data dispersion, so there's not much point in dealing with it. However, in inquiry investigation activities, in which students are dealing with messier real-world data, thinking about the dispersion of the data around the average is important.

Scientists have calculations of data dispersion that they use to help them interpret their graphs in figuring out statistics (some of which we discuss in Chapter 8, and we include worked-through examples and worksheets in the appendices so students can attempt to do these calculations). But in most cases, unless one is a pretty good senior student, the data dispersion calculations are too complicated.

However, as we argued in Chapter 1, there are advantages to having students deal with the information about data dispersion. It can help them deal with science as a probabilistic enterprise rather than a deterministic one; it can help them learn to use *hedging language* (okay,

---

3. We're not going to lie—we're going to do that re-mentioning stuff a lot. That's because we know what teachers are like. You're not going to read the whole book from front to back, you're going to read whatever chapter you think you need when you think you need it. So, we're going to mention important things, often in detail, in any chapter we think they're relevant to even *if* we've done it before because we don't want you to miss important stuff. We've both been classroom teachers, we know what it's like. For those of you reading from Chapter 1 onward who experience some repetition, we hope you're patient with our attempts to serve the needs of everyone and can treat it as a review.

we're getting ahead of ourselves here—that topic is discussed in Chapter 7); and it can help them get better at working with real-world data (which often has a lot of variation in it) to better understand what patterns exist even when there is some data scatter.

So, if the calculations are too complex for many students, what do we suggest? If we're arguing that students should better understand how dispersion can influence the conclusions drawn from graphs, then we must have *some* way to accomplish that. Well, we do. It's pretty simple actually—and you've already seen us do it. We suggest that you have your students graph the averages of the data (as they usually do) *and* the raw data on the graph. So, in other words, a bar graph in a student report should look like the one in Figure 1.6 (p. 10).

But there's a wee bit of a problem that teachers are going to face: graphing packages (such as Excel[4]) usually don't do graphing that way. They mostly work using averages and so forth to do the graphing. So, what's a teacher to do?

Well, what we do, as teachers, is have our students draw the graphs using a ruler, pencil, and graph paper and then plot the raw data on them. If you're bound and determined as a teacher to use graphing software, we'd suggest that you have the students plot the raw data on a printout of the graph and then provide an interpretation. To us it boils down to a simple question: Is it the science teacher's job to teach the student to use commercial software tools or is it his or her job to teach about science concepts and practices (including data literacy skills); and to teach about them in a

way that has students really understanding the underlying ideas so they can apply them to new situations they encounter?

We're pretty sure it's the second option, and we hope you think so too!

Predicting From Graphs

1. Bar Graphs: These graphs show the differences between the different category variables but cannot be used to predict what will happen with a new category. For instance, if a student rolled a marble into two types of cups—such as a paper and a plastic cup—to see how far they were pushed, he or she could not (from that activity) predict with any accuracy how far a Styrofoam cup would be pushed.

2. Line Graphs: These graphs cannot be used to predict with any strong accuracy any "new" categories that are added. For instance, if a student rolled marbles into different sized cups to see how far each was pushed, a new cup "in between" two of those cups in size would probably get pushed a distance between where the original two traveled, but exactly what distance cannot really be predicted. A cup smaller or bigger than the original cups will go farther or less far, but that's all that can be reasonably predicted— it is difficult to predict an actual distance.

3. Scatterplot Graphs: A trend line often shows the average relationship between two variables and can be used to predict one variable's outcome if you have the other. We're going to argue (later) that for students it's more useful to teach about trend bars because a trend bar can be used to predict a range within which an "in between" or "beyond" cup would be expected to travel. This is similar to calculating a formula for the line of best fit, with an error range, and using it with a new number of whole or partial cups. These graphs, and the "measure" data type, are the most powerful for use in science because they can make good predictions.

---

4. Programs, such as Excel, are created for knowledgeable adults to show data, particularly in business contexts. But that doesn't mean that those tools are great for teaching young students how to learn data literacy concepts or how to graph effectively. Those programs *might* also calculate those data dispersion statistics and show them automatically on the graphs, but that doesn't mean that they help the students really understand the concepts.

SCAFFOLDING STUDENTS TOWARD USING HIGHER-ORDER VARIABLES

In many cases, students designing a science investigation in schools are (implicitly) encouraged to design nominal-level studies. This does students a disservice for several reasons, including that they are learning about conducting science investigations in a way that is less common in science, and they are not engaging in an activity that can help develop higher-order thinking skills.

How might this be addressed?

Basically, teachers need to start encouraging students to do activities that have higher-order variables in them. That's not as difficult as it sounds because most basic nominal-level investigations can be scaffolded toward an ordinal or interval-ratio study.

Let's look at an example. One frequent study we've seen students do (over and over and over) is growing one plant on the counter and another in the dark to address the question, "Does the plant grow best in the light or dark?"

This study could be changed into an ordinal-level study by having three treatments (one plant on the counter, one plant hidden from light, and one plant that is in the light for the morning and in the dark for the afternoon)—or it could be one plant hidden from light, one plant in a paper bag in the light, and the other plant in the light without the paper bag.

The study could also be turned into an interval-ratio study by having each student group put their plant in the dark for different periods of time (one hour, two hours, three hours, and so on) and then compiling class data for analysis. In the first activity, most students would predict that the plant in the light will grow the best, in the second they're "pretty sure" the one in the light full time will grow the best, and in the third they are even less certain that the plant fully in the light will grow the best—especially if the teacher introduces the idea that plants might have optimal light-level preferences that may not be related to constant exposure.

In our experience, it requires just a bit more work to help students generate activities that use higher-order variables. The concept of "optimal" is one that is prevalent in biology, but it's hardly ever introduced to students in the classroom. Embedded in that concept of optimal is that an organism will have a range of responses to a stimulus, which is very different than them having only one reaction or another (which is a *nominal* view of nature).

Introducing students to studies with higher-order variables provides them with a more accurate perspective on how organisms (and other things) respond to a stimulus in nature. Far too often, students believe that outcomes from a study are polarized (such as a plant in dark versus light) rather than in some sort of a response range, and this misrepresents the types of relationships found in nature.

STUDENTS AND GRAPHING

Students often struggle with learning to draw and interpret graphs effectively. Here, we're going to briefly discuss two reasons that this can occur. Then in the following three chapters we'll discuss ideas about graphing each type of variable and present an activity for students that addresses the two main reasons students have trouble learning about graphing and graph interpretation.

Teachers often tell us that the math involved in creating graphs as a contributor to the difficulty students have in making and interpreting graphs. As a science teacher, you are primarily concerned about students learning the science and the concepts involved with graphing science data and not about teaching math. In the next few chapters, we're going to discuss how to get around this problem.

The second reason students sometimes have difficulty with graphing is the amount of abstraction they encounter (which can relate to the math issue). As a teacher, you may not even think about graphs as being abstract, but often graphs are constructed in a manner that is quite "experience distant" as far as the students are concerned (in other words, the data are not obviously and directly connected to an activity that the students engaged in). Sometimes we can do something about that in how we design the activities; at other times we have to rely on the effectiveness of previous instruction and activities. We suggest that having students learn graphing in a way in which there is little or no abstraction, in which there is a direct mapping of the actual experience to the data representation (i.e., the graph), helps them understand the graphing concepts better.

Let's look at an example: Imagine you are rolling a marble through a hole in an overturned paper cup and measuring how far the cup is pushed. On a full piece of paper, you've had your students draw a graph in which the vertical axis goes from 0 to 20 cm. One centimeter on the graph represents one centimeter that the cup has been pushed. That is a direct 1:1 mapping of the experience to the graph. There is little or no abstraction as far as the student is concerned because each tic on the graph represents the actual distance the cup moved (see the Direct Distance graph in Figure 2.1, p. 18). The student can visualize the cup moving.

Now imagine the students are going to do the graph differently. They draw a smaller graph, in which the vertical axis is labeled from 0 to 25 cm, but it is only 5 cm high. That means that each centimeter on the graph represents 5 cm that the cup has moved (see the Transformed Distance graph in Figure 2.1 for an example of this). Although adults may still be able to easily visualize this, for young students it represents a form of abstraction that makes it harder to make sense of what is going on—harder to understand the relationship between the distance the cup moved and, for instance, the type of cup.

The first example is "experience near," the second is more experience distant (of course, this is all relative—you could come up with examples that are even more experience distant). The first graph has a 1:1 mapping of the distance traveled by the cup and the distance indicated on the map. There is no transformation, no change. The second graph has a ratio transformation, and students have to visualize the cup traveling farther than the graph depicts.

The more experience distant the graph is from the data, the more difficulty students have learning the relationship between variables. If a teacher can have the graph drawn in a less experience-distant fashion, then they should use that as an approach to support student understanding.

Note that the units can also contribute to a graph being more experience distant. For example, a count is less abstract than a measure, whereas units for concepts such as velocity (m/s) or acceleration (m/s^2) are even more abstract or experience distant.

Thus, there are two ways graphs can move from being experience near (and easier for students to draw and interpret) to experience distant (or more abstract, and therefore more difficult to draw and interpret). Both ways relate to the degree to which the units are made

FIGURE 2.1

Examples of graphs that are on the trajectory from experience near to experience distant

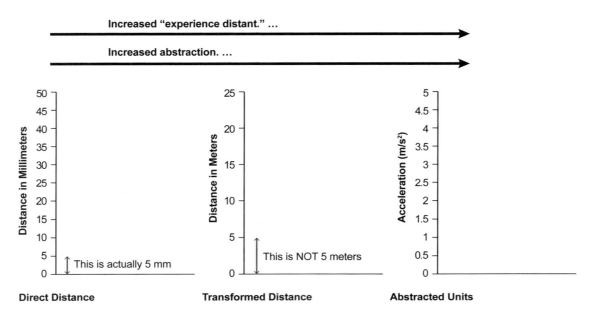

more abstract through (1) moving from a 1:1 relationship to being a ratio and (2) moving from being a direct distance measure (as in our examples in the following chapters and in Appendix II) to being a count, a measure, and finally a unit that involves more complex units (such as velocity or acceleration).

Learning how to use tables and graphs effectively should help students better engage in science investigations and will allow them to make appropriate decisions about which type of graph to use. Using the correctly formatted tables and the correct graphs lets students draw more accurate conclusions from the data they have collected.

Let's see what ideas we have to help students get better at making sense of data. In the next three chapters, we're going to further discuss each type of variable and provide example activities to help students learn concepts about the type of graph associated with each kind of variable and how to draw conclusions from it. (Other examples of activities that could teach about these graphing concepts are found in Appendix II.)

CHAPTER 3
DATA IN CATEGORIES: NOMINAL-LEVEL DATA

Data that are in categories without any obvious order or sequence are known as *nominal-level data*. As an example of nominal-level data, if a student wanted to compare the sleep habits of cats and dogs, the data she or he collected to compare their sleep habits would be at a nominal level.

Nominal data are usually recorded in a table as shown in Table 3.1.

TABLE 3.1

Example of how data are normally recorded in a table, using data on the number of hours dogs and cats sleep

Pet	Dogs sleeping	Cats sleeping
1	8	14
2	9	5
3	5	7
4	8	8
5	7	7
Avg.	7.4 hours/day	8.2 hours/day

Nominal-level data are often represented in a bar graph.[1] Although in some disciplines pie graphs are used with nominal data, they are much less common in science publications.

Data Literacy Comment 3.1: In science, data tables are usually structured so that the data can be inspected for patterns and trends as it is being collected. This inspection partly allows a judgment to be made about whether a particular value is a significant outlier (from the overall pattern) and thus whether the test may need to be redone (not an uncommon practice in science). Scientists sometimes say they "draw the graph in their head" when they look at data tables.

With the graph shown in Figure 3.1, a typical student interpretation would be completely consistent with the average shown in the data table, basically that cats sleep more than dogs sleep.

FIGURE 3.1

A graph comparing sleep amounts in common household pets

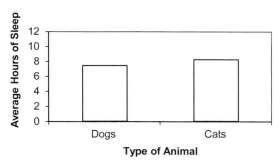

Comparing Sleep for Cats and Dogs

_____

1. Bar graphs are used for nominal values. If you see a *histogram*, it is basically a bar graph (1) without spaces between the bars, and (2) in which the categories on the horizontal axis are numeric (either numbers or ranges), and most frequently portraying frequency counts on the vertical axis. Histograms, therefore, are occasionally used in science with interval-ratio data (or ranges of interval-ratio data).

Now, let's take a look at the graph comparing cats and dogs if we put the raw data onto it (Figure 3.2).

FIGURE 3.2

A graph comparing sleep amounts in common household pets (showing raw data)

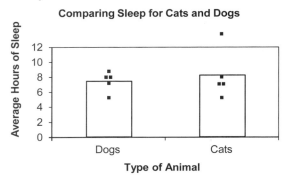

When we plot the raw data onto the graph, the graph looks different, and two things are obvious. First, there is an *outlier* cat who might really be distorting the arithmetic average for the cats overall. That one cat, perhaps a really old one, is *really* raising the average for the cat category. Second, even including that one outlier cat in the data set doesn't change something that becomes very clear when looking at the raw data: that the data for the cats overlaps that for the dogs quite a lot.

Data Literacy Comment 3.3: Science is a probabilistic discipline. In other words, it deals with probabilities. One problem with using bar graphs is that they do not (usually) represent the variation in the data. As a result, student interpretations are more often *absolute* or *deterministic*: "Cats sleep more than dogs." However, examining the data table reveals that all cats did not sleep more than all dogs. A more correct interpretation would be "On average, cats sleep more than dogs. Some days dogs sleep more than some cats."

Data Literacy Comment 3.2: Students often conduct the number of replicates for a study based on a number they are told by some authority figure. But this doesn't really represent what happens in science. The number of replicates in science is often based on considering (1) what is possible time- and money-wise, (2) a judgment made by the researcher on whether the (suspected) range of possible data has been adequately represented, and (3) if one's colleagues would accept the number of replicates as being adequate. There is no hard-and-fast number of replicates in science. You can find studies published with something being observed once (for instance, a type of animal behavior, such as lunge-feeding behaviors in whales) or you can find studies in which there are dozens and dozens of replicates (as with social behavior in small insects such as thrips).

Why is this overlap important? Because scientists draw their conclusions based on the means *and* the dispersion of the data around the means. If a statistical test was done on this data, it would probably conclude that there is no statistical difference between the amount of time cats and dogs sleep. This is different from the typical school science conclusion that would be reached that there *is* a difference between how much cats and dogs sleep because the means are different. In science, one usually only draws conclusions about means when the dispersion is considered.

Teaching Hint: You may help students reach qualified interpretations by asking them to put symbols on the graph for the raw data over top of where the bars are. This then helps the students recognize the data scatter around the average and makes it easier to get them to draw conclusions that take that data variation into account.

Teaching Hint: It is often difficult to get graphing packages to put raw data onto graphs. Remember, those packages are designed for adults and are designed for business purposes (which may be quite different from science ones). In many cases, hand-drawn graphs may help students develop better data literacy.

AN ACTIVITY TO TEACH ABOUT NOMINAL DATA AND HOW TO INTERPRET THEM

Bar graphs usually represent data that fall into different categories. In this activity[2] we'll use one each of a paper, plastic, and Styrofoam cup (of approximately the same size) for the different categories. So, the variable is "type of cup," which is a nominal-level variable.

Using an 11" × 17" piece of paper, draw a baseline about 10 cm from the bottom of the page (see Figure 3.3). Along the baseline, put three marks to represent the center of the leading edge of each of the three types of cups.

2. This activity, and others like it in the next two chapters, are the ones we've successfully presented at the national NSTA conventions for the last several years. We also offer variants of this activity in Appendix II that you can use to teach the same concepts.

Label the tics behind the line by the type of cup (Figure 3.3[a]).

FIGURE 3.3

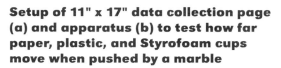

Setup of 11" x 17" data collection page (a) and apparatus (b) to test how far paper, plastic, and Styrofoam cups move when pushed by a marble

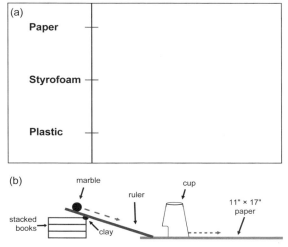

When the materials are set up as in Figure 3.3(b), have students place the first cup behind the line centered on the tic and align the ramp system behind the opening in the cup. At this point you might want to have the students describe the *controlled variables* (ones that stay the same all the time, such as where the marble is released from or where the end of the ruler is placed) and list those on the board.

You should then demonstrate collecting the data: Roll the marble down the ruler and into the cup and record with a pencil mark where the leading edge of the cup stops. Do this several times until you have a cluster of tics (see Figure 3.4, p. 22).

In our experience, once students have been walked through one example of recording tics or had it demonstrated from the front, they can work independently on collecting their own data. They should repeat the activity until they have completed it for all three types of cups.

FIGURE 3.4

Example of tics placed at where cup stopped

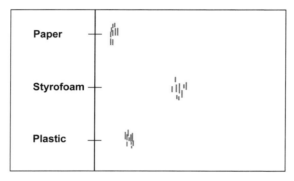

REPRESENTING THE DATA

Now the students can do a number of things to analyze the data. First, have them draw a circle that incorporates all, or at least most (see the inset on outliers[3]), of the data tics. Then have them place a large dot in the middle of the circle. This dot represents a type of average that approximates a median (or middle) value. When the students have completed this, the sheet of paper should look like the one in Figure 3.5(a).

The teacher can now introduce the concept of variation and how it exists because of natural differences in populations (such as variation in height within the class) or because of other variables that weren't being controlled effectively. In this example, you could have the students examine the lips of the cups. Often the lips have different shapes and feel different

when you run your finger along them. If the cup lips are examined with a hand lens, students will often identify that the paper and plastic cup lips are smooth, whereas the lip of the Styrofoam cup has a bit of texture. Ask the students to speculate about the effect of a smooth edge versus a rough one when sliding across a surface. Often the students' data will show that the circle for the Styrofoam cup is larger than that for the other types, and perhaps this roughness is why.

As the final step in representing the data, have your students take the ruler and place the middle of one end on the center dot in each circle with the other end extending vertically down to the baseline. Then have the students trace the outline of the ruler down to the baseline. When this is done, the sheet will now look like Figure 3.5(b).

Teaching Hint: Whenever any data collection is done, there are occasionally data points that lie away from other data points. These are called *outliers*. Sometimes this is part of normal variation (such as the one student in class that prefers vanilla ice cream over chocolate or some other kind). At other times this occurs because there are limits to how well the controlled variables can be controlled. Finally, an outlier may occur because another influence that no one had thought about is affecting the outcome. If this influence is identified, it becomes another (controlled) variable.

---

3. In the words of science teacher Lesley Rutledge, "Perhaps an outlier isn't really an outlier, and perhaps it is where 'different' science is happening (or the more exciting science is happening, in a lot of cases)."

FIGURE 3.5

Representing the data collected from the marble rolling activity

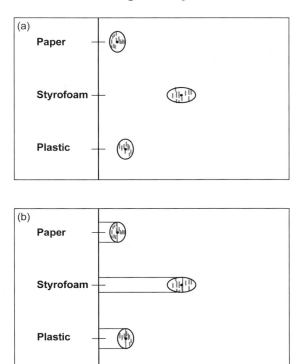

FIGURE 3.6

A rotated version of Figure 3.5 looks like a traditional bar chart

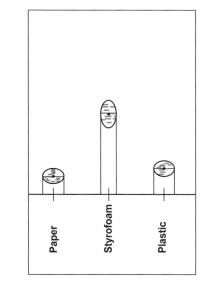

If you rotate the figure, it looks more like a traditional bar chart (Figure 3.6).

So, you can see that the students have created, without measuring, counting, numbers, mathematics or anything like that, a bar graph representing their data. Note that this bar graph is experience near, with a minimal level of abstraction (because the data and the graphical representation of it maps 1:1 onto the actual experience without any transformation at all).

INTERPRETING THE BAR GRAPH

Usually the data circles for the paper and plastic cup are a slightly different distance from the baseline, and the data circle of the Styrofoam cup is usually much farther from the baseline (and is also larger, representing greater variation in the data for that type of cup). Students typically approach interpreting the data by concluding that the different cups traveled different distances. This is consistent with how students are usually taught to interpret bar graphs that represent averaged data.

Teaching Hint: **"Stacking" the Environment.** The natural tendency of teachers is to make sure every student has the same size and types of cups so they all get the same answer. We'd like to argue you out of that approach in this type of activity. If students all have the same cups, then they're going to be comparing their answers with each other, which isn't really teaching them to argue from their own data.

What we suggest is "stacking" the environment. Have a selection of the different types of cups in different brands and sizes. It's even helpful for them to have sizes of the different types (plastic, Styrofoam, paper) close to each other, but not exact (so, basically, variables that you cannot control completely). This allows students to discuss how those slight differences might contribute to the differences in the distances the cups were pushed or in the data dispersion in their findings.

But is that what scientists would conclude? Determining which distances are significantly different from each other requires comparing both the distances and the amount of data variation. Thus, in this instance (as seen in Figure 3.6) the Styrofoam cup traveled a significantly farther distance from the baseline than did the paper or plastic cups. However, because of the amount of overlap of the plastic and paper cup data circles, it is more difficult to conclude that the paper and plastic cup traveled different distances. Therefore, a more scientifically correct conclusion would be that the Styrofoam cup traveled farther than the paper and plastic cups, but the paper and plastic cups slid more or less the same distance.

By having students do a comparison of the size of the circles and the amount of overlap, you're having them learn the foundations of analysis of variance (ANOVA) statistical tests (see Chapter 8). Drawing a conclusion like this is more scientifically accurate partly because it allows the use of what is called hedging language (see Chapter 7), which is used by scientists to indicate how certain they are about what they've figured out from their data.

LIMITATIONS TO THE DATA

Nominal-level data has limited predictive ability. For instance, in this example you can claim that Styrofoam cups travel farther when pushed than do plastic or paper cups. However, you cannot predict what would happen if you had *different* paper, plastic, or Styrofoam cups. Even if the cups were exactly the same size, there might be differences in how the paper or plastic or Styrofoam was made. So, often with nominal-level data and graphs you can describe what you found and what differences or similarities there were, but you are limited in your predictive ability for other situations. See *www.youtube.com/watch?v=5OrOhxoWlis* for a brief discussion of this topic.

CHAPTER 4
DATA IN ORDERED CATEGORIES: ORDINAL-LEVEL DATA

*O*rdinal-level data involve ordered categories—categories that have a sequence or order. An example of ordered categories would be dogs of different sizes. For instance, you might have access to some poodles, small Labrador retrievers, and Dobermans and want to know which breed could run the fastest between two points. The variable you would be interested in, in this case, would be the relationship between breed size and speed.

For ordinal data, the table would be made so that the dogs would be in order from smallest (poodle) to the largest (Doberman) breed (Table 4.1).

TABLE 4.1

Data collected to compare dog speeds

Trial	Poodle	Labrador	Doberman
1	14	17	8
2	13	10	9
3	13	16	6
4	15	8	8
5	17	9	7
Avg.	14.4 s	12.0 s	7.6 s

Note that the order does *not* mean that the the difference in size between the Labradors and poodles is the same as that between the Labradors and the Dobermans. The "gap" between them is not considered to be consistent.

Data Literacy Comment 4.1: Note that with this type of data, if you had a new dog that was in between Labradors and Dobermans in size, you could not predict what its speed would be with any accuracy, only that it would likely be in the range between the speed of the Labradors and Dobermans.

Ordinal-level data are most often represented in a line graph, although sometimes a bar graph is used. Usually, you can obtain more information from a line graph. The common way to graph ordinal data in science is shown in Figure 4.1.

FIGURE 4.1

An ordinal data graph example comparing dog breed speeds

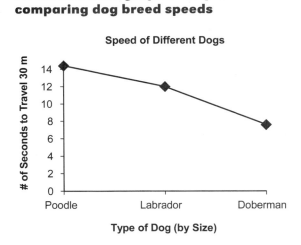

From a first look at the Figure 4.1 graph, it looks like the bigger (or taller) the dog breed is, the faster it can run. But is that the full story? What might the graph look like if it also had the raw data plotted on it? And how might that influence conclusions that a student might reach? Figure 4.2 depicts this.

FIGURE 4.2

An ordinal data graph example comparing dog breed speeds with raw data plotted on line graph

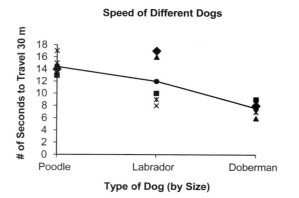

Speed of Different Dogs

Data Literacy Comment 4.2: Note that this type of graph also does not typically show the raw data. This leads to the same issues with student interpretations of the graph as was discussed in Chapter 3.

With the raw data plotted on the line graph, the wider variation in the times of the Labrador dogs is immediately obvious. One could then ask a student why such a variation might be found. (One possible answer is that Labradors often retrieve hunting prey that they haven't seen fall, so they move back and forth looking for it instead of traveling in a straight line. Thus, Labradors might travel between one point and another differently because they were bred to do that.)

Does this change your conclusions any? It depends on what observations were made during the time trials the dogs ran. On average, Doberman dogs clearly travel faster than the other two breeds, but it's harder to make a determination about the poodle and Labrador breeds because information about how straight the dog ran is also needed—and that would be a new variable. It sounds like another study is necessary if that qualitative information wasn't recorded in the first study.

Teaching Hint: Note that it was both a lot of work and complicated to show a joined line only for the average (using commonly used graphing software)—more than many high school students could handle. As suggested earlier, students might initially learn better data literacy skills hand drawing such graphs. If you move to graphing software later, you could have the software do the "joined line" based on the average, and then have the students add the raw data by hand.

AN ACTIVITY TO TEACH ABOUT ORDINAL DATA AND HOW TO INTERPRET IT

Line graphs are different than bar graphs because they usually represent an independent variable that follows an order; for example, small, medium, large, and extra large (in other words, the items on the *x*-axis are related to each other in an ordered way). If you've collected a variety of cups (as suggested in the Stacking the Environment inset in the previous chapter), take a look at the cups. Even when you are looking at cups from the same source (such as a coffee shop) you'll notice that the difference in size between the small and the medium cup isn't necessarily the same as that between the medium and the large cup, which is why it's just an ordered-category data type of graph. Of course, if you had the actual measured volume of the cup you would be dealing with interval-ratio data (see Chapter 5).

So, given that line graphs usually represent data that falls into ordered categories, for this activity[1] students will obtain four cups of different sizes but made of the same material (plastic, paper, or Styrofoam).[2] Have the students put four equally spaced tics across the data baseline (Figure 4.3). Make sure they leave enough space for the cup to move around a bit without going over the edge of the paper (half a cup–width extra from the side should be enough).

FIGURE 4.3

Example setup of 11" x 17" data page for the ordinal data cup experiment

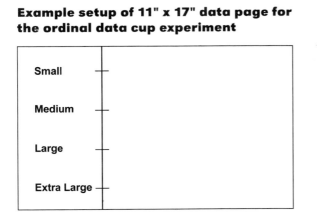

---

1. This activity and the others like it in the following and preceding chapter are the ones we've successfully presented at the national NSTA convention for the last number of years. We also offer variants of this activity in Appendix II.

2. Note that in keeping with our Stacking the Environment comment in the previous chapter, we suggest that the cups come from at least a couple of different manufacturers. This gives other variables for students to identify that they can use to explain the variation, such as lip width, the presence of wax, static attraction, and so on.

FIGURE 4.4

Examples of recording of data tics (a), circles or ovals being placed around data tics (b), and a center dot placed in the circle or oval (i.e., median) (c)

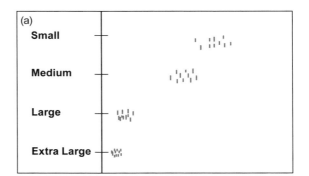

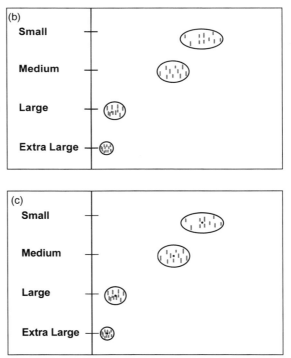

Have the students collect their data (setup is the same as in Figure 4.3), going from the smallest cup to the largest cup (Figure 4.4[a]), and then, in the same way as described in the previous chapter, have them draw the data circles (Figure 4.4[b]), and finally have them place the dot in the center (Figure 4.4[c])—but have them stop there.

> *Teaching Hint*: You'll notice that the graph has a wider scatter of tics for the small cup. You might get the students to try and figure out why. Basically, the lip has a greater chance to catch on protuberances from the paper and rough spots the more paper it travels over. Also, with a small cup, the marble striking the cup can make it "roll" on the edge from side to side a bit more.

At this point in the activity, a short review by the teacher might be useful in helping students understand the differences between nominal and ordinal data.

We suggest noting the following on the blackboard (or PowerPoint):

1. Bar graphs are used when the data are in distinct categories. Bar graphs have vertical lines.

2. Line graphs are used when the data are one category but one with a rough order to it. Line graphs are joined by a line.

You might want to have a short discussion about these issues with the students regarding how line graphs allow you to get an idea about patterns or trends, which is what scientists attempt to find when they study variables.

Then have the students join the center dots together with a ruler from left to right on their data sheets (Figure 4.5).

FIGURE 4.5

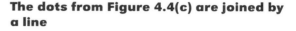

The dots from Figure 4.4(c) are joined by a line

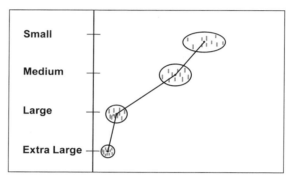

You might find rotating the graph 90 degrees helpful in assisting the students in interpreting the graph (Figure 4.6).

FIGURE 4.6

Rotated graph depicting the effect of cup size on the distance the marble pushes the cup

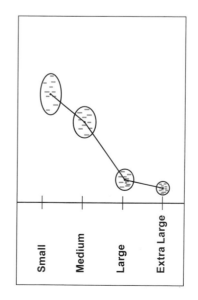

Rotating the graph makes it a bit easier to analyze. Now you can see that what the students have created—without measuring, counting, numbers, mathematics, or anything like that—is a line graph representing their data. Note that this line graph is experience near with a minimal level of abstraction (because the data maps 1:1 onto the actual experience without any transformation at all).

INTERPRETING THE LINE GRAPH

The data in this diagram can be analyzed on a couple of different levels. The first level of analysis is the level of the cups, or the level of the raw observation alone. This is the type of conclusion you might expect lower to middle grades to reach. So, the first *general* conclusion is that "smaller cups are pushed farther than larger cups." But this statement can be refined into one that conveys more information about the data in the graph. More specifically, you could conclude that "there is a relationship between the size of the cup and the distance it is pushed." Note that this is more of a generalized statement in relation to the variables that are being studied (i.e., cup size and distance).

In science, relationships that "decrease" from left to right are often thought of as *negative* relationships, and those that "increase" from left to right are thought of as *positive* relationships. Also note that since sizes of the cups were not uniformly different (nor will they be in your classes), it was a bit of a rough pattern; it was not a smooth straight line or curved line. This pattern is to be expected.

Given that the distance the cups travel decreases from left to right, the second restating of the conclusion could be refined to say, "There is a negative relationship between cup size and the distance the cup was pushed." In

other words, the bigger the cup, the less distance it was pushed.

This is a good conclusion, but notice that it is dealing with the raw observations of a physical phenomena that occurred because we chose cups of different sizes. However, apart from their size, the cups often have other different features. For instance, the diameters of the rim might be different between the cups, the rims might be coated with wax in some cases and not others, or the rim might be square on some cups and rounded on others.

But one thing that we *can* be reasonably certain about with cups of the same materials is that the masses of the cups are different, with the mass increasing from small to big cups (left to right on the graph). So, really, a more complex conclusion that can be reached from Figure 4.6 is that "there is a negative relationship between mass (of the cups) and the distance the cups were pushed."

Of course, it's not necessarily a smooth relationship; you can see that it is kind of a messy and staggered (sort of curved?) relationship because of the cups we chose (each with slightly different features), but *in general* as the mass of the cups increases the distance they travel decreases.

Is that what scientists would conclude? As we've mentioned before, drawing conclusions about what distances are significantly different from each other requires comparing both the distances and the amount of data variation. Thus, in this instance we cannot be sure if the distance hasn't plateaued with the large and extra-large cup because of the amount of overlap of the circles. However, it is probably safe to say, from a science perspective, that the cups traveled significantly different distances from the small to the medium to the large cup.

By having students do a comparison of the size of the circles and the amount of overlap, you're having them learn the foundations of the analysis of variance (ANOVA) statistical tests (see Chapter 8). Drawing a conclusion like this is more scientifically accurate partly because the conclusion allows the use of what is called hedging language (see Chapter 7), which is used by scientists to indicate how certain they are about the conclusions they are drawing from their data.

LIMITATIONS TO THE DATA

Ordinal-level variables are higher order than nominal variables because they allow you to make some predictions based on the pattern obtained (no predictions are possible if there is no pattern in the data). For instance, if you had a new cup that was between the medium and the large cup in size, then you could predict with some certainty that it would travel a distance that was between the two but not with any certainty exactly where. If you want more accuracy in estimating the distance of the new cup, you'd have to perhaps standardize the diameter and width of the lip, the height, and so forth and only change the mass variable.

Hmm, perhaps that variable—mass—should be isolated so that we could have a better understanding of the relationship between pushed distance and mass. Of course, if we did that, if we adjusted *only* the mass in some kind of a consistent fashion, then we'd be dealing with another sort of variable: the interval-ratio variable type. We'll discuss that variable type in the next chapter.

CHAPTER 5
MEASURED DATA: INTERVAL-RATIO-LEVEL DATA

nterval-ratio-level data are those for which there are direct measures that are proportional against a consistent scale. For instance, the distance from 15 m to 20 m is exactly the same as that from 30 m to 35 m. That seems quite straightforward doesn't it? This kind of data also includes direct counts, such as number of carrots. Interval-ratio data variables are the most common type found in science.

In the following example using a paper helicopter (see Figure 5.1 for instructions), the unit of weight is the number of paper clips attached to the bottom of the helicopter. In using the number of paper clips as a unit of weight, we are taking interval-ratio measures because two paper clips are exactly twice the weight of one paper clip, and four paper clips are twice the weight of two paper clips.

The research question for the helicopter project is, "In what way does the number of paper clips affect the drop time?"

FIGURE 5.1

Details on cutting out a paper helicopter

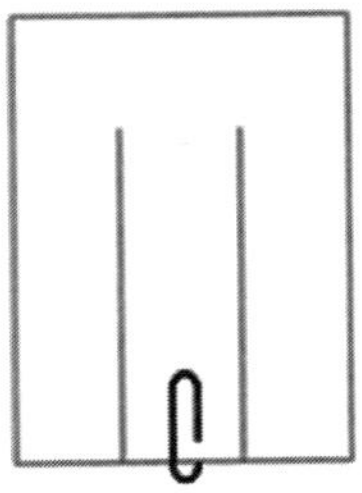

Instructions: Cut up the lines on each side of the paper clip and lightly fold horizontally (in opposite directions) at the top of each cut) to create the blades. The piece of paper is 9 cm wide and 12 cm high.

Interval-ratio data of this type are often represented in a table designed like Table 5.1.

TABLE 5.1

Example data table for interval-ratio data

Trial	1 Paper clip	2 Paper clips	3 Paper clips	4 Paper clips
1	2.19	2.03	1.68	1.45
2	2.00	1.90	1.55	1.40
3	2.04	1.95	1.60	1.33
4	2.13	2.00	1.71	1.29
5	2.09	1.87	1.65	1.38
Avg.	2.09 s	1.95 s	1.64 s	1.37 s

This is really a table that has this general design shown in Table 5.2.

TABLE 5.2

Example blank table for discrete interval-ratio data

Trial	X1	X2	X3	X4
1	Y	Y	Y	Y
2	Y	Y	Y	Y
3	Y	Y	Y	Y
4	Y	Y	Y	Y
5	Y	Y	Y	Y
Avg.				

Why might this data table design (Table 5.1) work well in this particular case?

If you remember, earlier we mentioned scientists "drawing a graph in their heads" when they look at data as they collect it. In this particular case, designing the table in a multi-column manner made it somewhat easier to draw the graph in your head. If this data were put into a traditional *x-y* data table (as in Table 5.3), then it would be harder to draw the graph in your head. See if you can visualize a graph in your head from a data table structured the way it is in Table 5.3.

TABLE 5.3

A more traditional data table design for *x-y* (interval-ratio) data

Paper clips	Time
1	2.19
1	2.00
1	2.04
1	2.13
1	2.09
2	2.03
2	1.90
2	1.95
2	2.00
2	1.87
3	1.68
3	1.55
3	1.60
3	1.71
3	1.65
4	1.45
4	1.40
4	1.33
4	1.29
4	1.38

Of course, we can use that first table design with this type of data because the *cause variable* (the one that would go on the *x*-axis of the graph) is in distinct categories (even though it is a measure, the measure is in distinct categories), in this case, multiple measures of one through four paper clips. If the *x-axis variable* were also a measure for which there were no distinct categories (for example, if you were examining the relationship between arm length and leg length), then you would have to use the more traditional *x-y* data table from which it would be harder to draw a graph in your head. The point is, if students can use a table with a design that encourages drawing a graph in their heads, then it is more like the practices of scientists. In other words, using a table like that is more like *working and thinking like a scientist*.

So, if scientists draw a graph from *x-y* data, what kind of graph do they draw? In science, it is most usual to graph interval-ratio data using an *x-y* graph (also called a scatterplot; Figure 5.2).

FIGURE 5.2

Example interval-ratio graph in which the *x*-axis data are in distinct categories

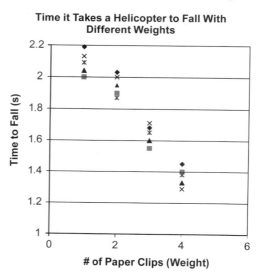

INTERPRETING *X-Y* GRAPHS

You might note that the graph for a study such as this one (with the paper clip weights) looks somewhat like the previous line graph. But there are several differences. First, it is possible to predict between individual measures with some reasonable accuracy. This would be teaching your students about *interpolation* (predicting between measured points). They could do this by estimating how quickly the helicopter would drop if it were weighted with two and a half paper clips. Then, with some work, they could test their prediction.

You can also predict beyond what was measured and then test that prediction. In this case, the students could predict, using the graph, what the drop time would be for five paper clips and then test the drop time to see if their prediction was correct. Predicting from one's data in this way is called *extrapolation* (predicting beyond the measured points).

How does one use a graph to predict? to interpolate? to extrapolate? In most situations students are taught about using a *line of best fit*.

Data Literacy Comment 5.1: Earlier we mentioned the issue of science being thought of deterministically as opposed to probabilistically. How might having students learn to predict from a line of best fit contribute to their developing deterministic perspectives on science?

So, now we'll look at the graph depicting a paper helicopter weighted with different numbers of paper clips (each of which weighs about 1 g) and make a prediction from it.

First, we drew a line of best fit by hand (notice that it wasn't a straight line). Next, we drew a vertical line on it going up from two and a half paper clips to allow us to *interpolate* how quickly the helicopter would fall if it were weighted with two and a half paper clips. Last, we drew a line horizontally across from where the vertical line intersected the line of best fit to intersect the effect line (where we can read the estimated amount of time it would take) (Figure 5.3).

FIGURE 5.3

Predicting data from a trend line

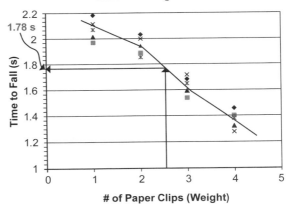

Using that approach, we can see the estimate that it would take 1.78 s for the helicopter to fall if it was weighted with two and a half paper clips.

How likely do you think it would be 1.78 s if you tested it? How many times would you have to test it to get a measure of 1.78 s? You might decide that you had to measure it a few times and take an average, but given the slight "bend" in the graph, even then are you certain that it would be 1.78 s?

If a student makes predictions using that approach, they are predicting from a *single value* that they will get a *single value*. By doing this, they see science as coming up with absolute answers—that science is deterministic within very narrow boundaries. This, of course, is not the way of science.

How can this thought process be avoided?

> *Data Literacy Comment 5.2*: When scientists analyze a data set, their analysis includes calculating how well a line (or model) fits the data by taking into account the variation in the data (for example, by generating an *r*-squared value). When scientists interpret their graphs, they do so while considering the variation in the data by thinking about those measures. When they make estimates or predictions using statistics associated with the graph, they usually estimate the *range* that their prediction will fall in or take into account statistical indications of that range.

How might those implicit learning outcomes be changed if students were able to predict a range of possible outcomes for two and a half paper clips? A range in which they were "pretty darned sure' what the helicopter drop speed would be? Would that still generate the perspective that there was a single right answer? Or would it help them take a more probabilistic view of science claims?

Figure 5.4 is an example of a graph with a *trend bar* drawn on it (which is really just an uncalculated confidence interval, one of the types of calculated measures of error used by scientists) instead of a line of best fit (which schools traditionally teach). When a student makes a prediction using a trend bar, they obtain a *range* of possible outcomes for their

prediction rather than just a single value. Determining a range of predicted outcomes using this approach better approximates the way in which scientists work and better conveys that science findings are probabilistic.

> *Teaching Hint*: We have successfully used this approach with students in grade 7 (and up) to teach how to make predictions about possible ranges of outcome. Teachers sometimes tell us that they're not sure their students could understand this approach, but our success with the activity has been with average students.

FIGURE 5.4

Demonstrating the use of a trend bar for prediction

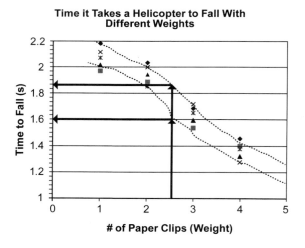

Time it Takes a Helicopter to Fall With Different Weights

From this graph, a student could predict that they were "pretty darned sure" that a helicopter with two and a half paper clips would hit the ground between 1.61 and 1.87 s.

Using this approach reinforces that science is probabilistic, that it is used to predict the most likely outcomes, and that those outcomes might be within a range.

AN ACTIVITY TO TEACH ABOUT INTERVAL-RATIO DATA AND HOW TO INTERPRET IT

Scatterplot graphs are different than the other two types because the variables of both axes are measures. Whereas in the nominal and ordinal data types the x-axis was indicated by categories, in the case of interval-ratio data both the x- and y-axis have measures with units on them.

In this activity[1] the students examine how far stacks of one, two, three, four, and five cups are pushed (Figure 5.5), which, because the cups are the cause variable, will be on the x-axis. Notice that two cups weigh twice as much as one cup, four cups weigh twice as much as two cups, and so on. This data type is different than the ordered category, which doesn't necessarily have the same measurement gaps between different sizes of cups. In other words, the difference between a small and a medium cup might be quite different than the difference between a large and an extra-large cup, and therefore the cup sizes represent ordinal-level data, whereas in interval-ratio data the increases are by the same *consistent* ratio.

FIGURE 5.5

How to set up the cups for collecting the x-axis data

In this activity, have the students get five cups of the same size and material. Have them put five equally spaced tics across the data baseline (Figure 5.6). Because the cups are being stacked in this activity, one cup is the equivalent of a "mass unit." For instance, one could think of it as how far a marble pushes a cup that weighs 10, 20, 30, 40, or 50 g.

FIGURE 5.6

Data collection sheet setup for the cup experiment

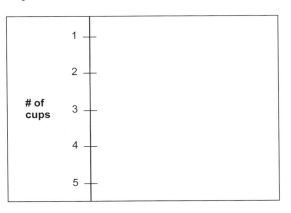

Have the students collect data for one, two, three, and four cups (Figure 5.7[a], p. 36). At this point they should draw the circle around the tics (Figure 5.7[b], p. 36).

---

1. This activity, and the others like it in the preceding two chapters, are the ones we've successfully presented at the national NSTA convention for the last several years. We also offer variants of this activity in Appendix II that you can use to teach the same concepts.

FIGURE 5.7

Examples of recording data tics (a), circles being placed around the data tics (b), and center dots (i.e., median) being placed in the circle (c).

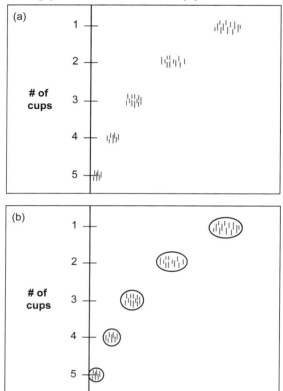

approach: Have the students draw a trend bar (see Figure 5.7[c]) that takes into account the variation in the data. For a trend line, professional scientists calculate an *r*-squared value (which measures how well the line represents the measured data; see Chapter 8), and when they make predictions from the graph they think about the variation in the data.

In looking at the graph in Figure 5.7[c], it might be difficult to make an interpretation because of its orientation. Remember, normally in science the treatment or cause (or in science speak, independent variable) is on the *x*-axis. So, to help make it easier to interpret the graph, we'll rotate it 90 degrees. This will make the orientation of the graph of the data we collected consistent with the scientific conventions of having the cause variable on the horizontal axis (Figure 5.8).

FIGURE 5.8

A rotated graph depicting the effect of the number of stacked cups on the distance the marble pushes the cup

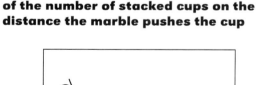
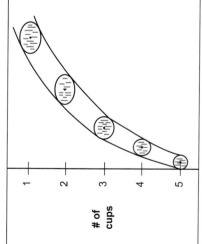

As discussed earlier, although it is common in classrooms to have students draw trend lines or lines of best fit, we suggest using a different

Aha! This now looks a bit more like a traditional scatterplot (i.e., cause on the horizontal axis, effect on the vertical axis) and is a bit easier to interpret. A simple interpretation of this graph would be that there is a consistent pattern of how far the cup was pushed by the marble.

> *Teaching Hint:* **Testing Predictions.**
> Students often predict linear relationships when they're asked to make a prediction of how far five cups would go on the basis of collecting data on one cup. From a teaching perspective, having them collect information on one and two cups and then making a prediction that they test (with three or more cups) can be useful so that students learn by hands-on experience that many relationships in science are not linear.

A more complex interpretation might call the relationship in Figure 5.8 *curvilinear*, or curved, and might note that the distance five cups was pushed was a *lot* less than only 20% of the distance one cup was pushed (if it was a proportional relationship, you would think it would drop by even ratios: two cups half the distance of one cup, three cups one-third the distance of one cup, and so on). You could use this idea to predict how far partial cup weights (e.g., one and a half cups) could be pushed (and later add this weight by sticking putty to the cup).

> *Teaching Hint:* **Dealing With Confounding Variables.** Although students think about obvious controlled variables, they often miss nonobvious ones, and it can be up to the teacher to bring those to their attention. In this activity if we were working with older students, we would point out that the pattern of the cups as they were stacked might be influenced by a change in center of mass. We would propose that maybe *that* variable, the center of mass not being constant, is what was causing the curve, and we would ask them to prove that it wasn't a change in the center of mass that was causing the curve in the trend bar.

WHAT IF THE INTERVAL-RATIO DATA ARE NOT DISCRETE?

The above example using stacked cups represents a particular type of interval-ratio data because the *x*-axis data are discrete (i.e., whole-numbers) and fall into a regular pattern across the *x*-axis. However, there are many, many types of interval-ratio data that are not discrete on the *x*-axis. For instance, what if you wanted to compare the relationship between arm length and leg length in your class? This type of relationship is useful, for instance, to archaeologists who find an arm bone and from it want to estimate the height of the individual (through estimating leg length).

This type of relationship (which is not a causal relationship but a correlational relationship) gives different data patterns (such as depicted in Figure 5.9, p. 38) than the previous example. Figure 5.9 depicts four different data

FIGURE 5.9

Examples of different types of scatterplot relationships

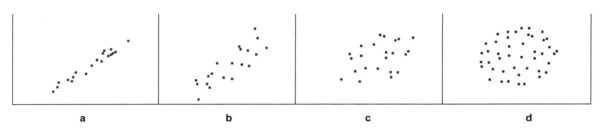

| a | b | c | d |

distributions you might find in a scatterplot in which both variables are interval-ratio measures (many others would lie between those examples).

Note that graphs (a) to (c) depict relationships (between the variables on the *x*- and *y*-axes) for which scientists would claim you can see that the variable on the vertical axis changes with the variable on the horizontal axis—that there is a significant relationship. If you were going to make a prediction using a trend bar, then predictions on the vertical axis would involve a narrower range in graph (a) than in graph (c). This indicates what scientists would refer to as *different strengths of relationships between the two variables*. In this example graph, (a) has a stronger relationship between the two variables than the variables portrayed in graph (c). Note that a weaker relationship doesn't mean it's not important—it might mean there are variables that haven't been considered yet that are creating scatter in the data.

However, studies of students who have learned about trend lines and who have examined the strong relationships present in textbooks have made an interesting finding. Those students (likely most students) report that there is only a relationship portrayed in graphs that look like (a) and, unlike scientists, conclude that there *not* a relationship in graphs

that are like those in (b) and (c). So, effectively, students seem to be learning that unless relationships between variables are almost perfect, they're not worth paying attention to.

Both of us think that this is a very dangerous message to teach students because relationships in the real world are hardly ever as strong as that shown in graph (a). Much environmental and social data are more like the data in graphs (b) and (c).

Finally, we'll point out that we haven't discussed the scatterplot seen in (d) yet. In that scatterplot, no pattern is apparent (in other words, you could draw a trend line through it in almost any direction and the average distance of data points from the line would be about the same).

CAUSALITY VERSUS CORRELATIONAL RELATIONSHIPS

A frequent error made by students in interpreting graphs is that they claim that a correlational relationship (in which one variable changes consistently with the other) in their data *is* a causal relationship (in which one variable is *causing* the other to change). Science makes a careful distinction between a correlational versus a causal relationship, and it is important not to confuse them (see Data Literacy Comment 5.3).

Let's examine a real world example looking at the relationship between the arm and leg lengths of students in a grade 7 class as depicted in Figure 5.10. (The raw data for this graph is discussed in Table 6.6, p. 44.)

FIGURE 5.10

A scatterplot depicting the relationship between arm length and leg length in teenagers

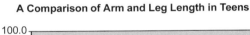

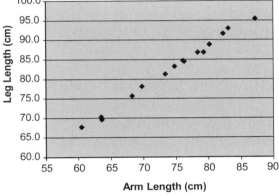

Notice that this is *not* a causal graph because arm length doesn't cause leg length nor the reverse. Both are probably influenced by common genetics, nutrition, and so on. That means that this is a correlational graph, so either leg length or arm length could be the *x*-value. The choice of which length to put on which axis is entirely arbitrary in this type of graph.

So, what kind of correlation exists? First, it's a positive relationship (as one increases in value so does the other). Second, it is a very strong correlation because all of the data points lie very close to the line of best fit (in this case a straight line). If we were to calculate the slope of the line, we would find that it is reasonably close to 0.9, which is the normal relationship between arm length and leg length as one approaches adulthood.

Because of this strong relationship (and others in relation to total body length and so forth), it is relatively easy for anthropologists to use data tables similar to this to help match bones to the correct bodies at archaeological digs or crime scenes (such as mass graves).

Data Literacy Comment 5.3: It cannot be emphasized enough that in science a *correlational* relationship does not mean that it is a *causal* relationship (where one variable causes another to change). Establishing causality has been a debate among philosophers for hundreds of years, but a few simple rules might help:
1. Temporal precedence: The cause has to happen *before* the effect. It's pretty hard to say that one thing causes another when it hasn't happened yet.
2. The cause and effect covary: When one changes the other one also changes, and the change of the following one has to be in some kind of a pattern (in other words, not like graph Figure 5.9[d]).
3. No other plausible alternatives: You have to rule out that the effect isn't actually being influenced by some other variable, including one that might also be influencing what you think the cause variable is.

CHAPTER 6
STRUCTURING AND INTERPRETING DATA TABLES

The data tables present in science articles are not necessarily structured the same way as those used by scientists as they collect their data. When doing research with scientists, Mike noticed that the structure of data tables used by scientists as they collected their data had an obvious feature: they were designed to "map onto" the types of graphs they planned on using to show their data. Scientists, when asked to talk about what they did when looking at raw data (found in tables or maps) commented that they "drew a graph in their head" as they looked at the data—even while collecting it.

This highlights two things. First, it shows how important proper table design is because some layouts make it easier to draw graphs in your head than others. Second, it demonstrates that scientists are trying to make sense of their data *as they collect it*, not just when they finish collecting it. It's safe to say that scientists think about their data and patterns in it constantly, to the point that they sometimes revise research projects partway through to allow them to get more and, in their view, better data.

DATA TABLES ARE A FORM OF MEMORY

Anthropologists who study workplace environments report that effective work environments are often designed to help the employee do a better job.[1] In a similar way,

studies of scientists by anthropologists report that the data table design acts as a cue to remind scientists to gather specific types of data. Research studies are often complex, with many different activities going on at once. The anthropological studies of scientists suggest that a properly designed data table will help students collect their data more effectively. After all, if it works for scientists why shouldn't it be helpful for students?

NOMINAL AND ORDINAL VARIABLE TABLES

Nominal or ordinal data tables can have as few as two columns. In our example below (Table 6.1), we have four data columns and a column that shows the number of trials or replicates.

TABLE 6.1

Dog speed data without sorting the columns on the basis of dog size

Trial	Poodle	Labrador	Doberman	Schnauzer
1	14	17	8	10
2	13	10	9	8
3	13	16	6	9
4	15	8	8	11
5	17	9	7	9
Avg.	14.4 s	12 s	7.6 s	9.4 s

In examining this table, we should ask what conclusions we can draw from the data while

---

1. A well-known study by Hutchins (Hutchins, E. 1995. How a cockpit remembers its speeds. *Cognitive Science* 19 (3): 265–288) demonstrated how the design of the cockpit interacted with pilot's actions so that the pilots flew the plane more effectively because they could better remember to do things that were necessary.

it is still only in the table (before we graph it). Tables are a form of summarizing data, and there's nothing wrong with moving information around to try and see what patterns there are.

In the first version of the table above (Table 6.1), neither the dog size nor the average times are in any particular order. What happens if we move columns around to correspond to some average? In Table 6.2, we sorted the columns by average time over 30 m.

TABLE 6.2

Dog speed data after sorting the columns based on average time

Trial	Poodle	Labrador	Schnauzer	Doberman
1	14	17	10	8
2	13	10	8	9
3	13	16	9	6
4	15	8	11	8
5	17	9	9	7
Avg.	14.4 s	12 s	9.4 s	7.6 s

Now that the table is sorted by average speed, we can look at the dog breeds and see if there's any pattern. Hmm, do you see any? You could look at trends in dog size. It was a pretty big schnauzer (bigger than a poodle), but it was a lot faster than the Labrador over the 30 m. Perhaps you needed to record *how* it ran that 30 m. But if you only had the table, is there anything else you could notice?

You might look at the ratios between the highest and lowest time values for each breed. If you did that, you'd notice that for the Labrador the longest time was more than twice the shortest time (17 s vs. 8 s). That's a *lot* of variation compared to the other dog breeds

(which were 17:13, 11:8, and 9:7 s). Are all dogs the same? How can we explain that difference? If you read about the four different breeds, you'd find that three of them (poodle, schnauzer, and Doberman) are target or prey oriented and therefore run at targets. Labrador retrievers, on the other hand, as part of their breed's behaviour repertoire, range back and forth to find what they're retrieving … and if you're ranging back and forth, you run between two points more slowly.

Note that designing and then reformulating the table so that its averages lie along a horizontal line is similar to how nominal and ordinal data would be graphed, and therefore it is easier to visualize the comparisons even before you actually draw a graph.

INTERVAL-RATIO VARIABLE TABLES

In Chapter 5 we discussed the basics of how tables are organized for interval-ratio variables. First, we'll review Chapter 5 a bit, and then we'll work through an example.

Basically, there are two data table designs used for interval-ratio data, depending on whether the cause (or independent) variable is *discrete* or not. What does this mean? Discrete data falls into specific categories and not between them (e.g., numbers of paper clips, height in centimeters only, number of stacked cups), and are usually a whole number, usually with multiple measures at each of those discrete categories (Figure 5.2, p. 32, showing Time It Takes a Helicopter to Fall With Different Weights is a good example of this). The other type of data is *nondiscrete* (or continuous), in which the cause variable is a measure that is constituted from either whole or real numbers. Those data sets result in graphs such as the one shown in Figure 5.9 (p. 38).

Decisions about how to structure tables to collect interval-ratio data are based on the idea that one wants to visually inspect the data for patterns as it is being collected. This visual inspection can be as simple as looking for rough patterns (when one number goes up the other goes down consistently) or may involve actually picturing graphs with data points on them—something that studies of scientists doing their research found that they do.

If the interval-ratio variable has discrete measurements, which means basically the treatments (i.e., things you are changing to see what happens) are in whole numbers and in sequential order (such as the number of paper clips on the bottom of a paper helicopter), then you have a table design that looks like Table 6.3.

TABLE 6.3

Example of a blank table for discrete interval-ratio data

Trial	X1	X2	X3	X4
1	Y	Y	Y	Y
2	Y	Y	Y	Y
3	Y	Y	Y	Y
4	Y	Y	Y	Y
5	Y	Y	Y	Y
Avg.				

This allows you to examine the averages across the bottom to see if there are patterns. For instance, look at the paper helicopter data you saw, shown in Table 6.4.

TABLE 6.4

Effect of the number of paper clips on helicopter fall time (s)

Trial	1 Paper clip	2 Paper clips	3 Paper clips	4 Paper clips
1	2.19	2.03	1.68	1.45
2	2.00	1.90	1.55	1.40
3	2.04	1.95	1.60	1.33
4	2.13	2.00	1.71	1.29
5	2.09	1.87	1.65	1.38
Avg.	2.09 s	1.95 s	1.64 s	1.37 s

Notice that if you look across the bottom, as the number of paper clips increases from left to right, the time for the helicopter to fall declines. It's not clear how consistent the pattern is, but there does seem to be a rough decline as it goes from left to right.

Designing the table that way accomplished the goal of having a table that allowed you to visually inspect your data for patterns. This data would then be portrayed in a graph such as that in Figure 5.2 (p. 32), which allows you to determine the consistency of the pattern.

If the interval-ratio variable is nondiscrete (in other words the x-variable has values that are not whole numbers), then the data table usually has the general format of Table 6.5 (p. 44).

TABLE 6.5

Basic interval-ratio data table format

	x-variable	y-variable
Replicate 1		
Replicate 2		
Replicate 3		
Replicate 4		
Replicate 5		
Replicate 6		
...		

If we look at arm- and leg-length data for teens in an x-y table as it is being collected, we see the following (Table 6.6):

TABLE 6.6

Arm- and leg-length data for teens

Arm (cm)	Leg (cm)
69.8	78.1
73.4	81.3
76.1	84.7
78.4	86.8
79.3	86.8
60.5	67.7
68.3	75.7
82.3	91.6
80.2	88.8
63.6	69.6
83.1	93.0
76.3	84.5
74.8	83.3
63.5	70.3
87.2	95.4

Note that the x-variable numbers aren't in order. One of the first things students can do is to put the table in order by one variable or the other (usually it's by the first column). Doing so can help with drawing a graph in one's head. If we do that with the arm- and leg-length data, we get a table that looks like Table 6.7.

TABLE 6.7

Arm- and leg-length data for teens sorted by arm length

Arm (cm)	Leg (cm)
60.5	67.7
63.5	70.3
63.6	69.6
68.3	75.7
69.8	78.1
73.4	81.3
74.8	83.3
76.1	84.7
76.3	84.5
78.4	86.8
79.3	86.8
80.2	88.8
82.3	91.6
83.1	93.0
87.2	95.4

Notice that now the table can be more easily visually inspected for patterns. If you look at the table in which the left column is in order, you can now scan down from top to bottom and see that in all cases as the arm length gets greater so does the leg length (you're probably not very surprised at that, but other data sets may not be so tidy).

As you saw in Figure 5.10 (p. 39), the arm- and leg-length data fell into a reasonably straight line when graphed. In this particular case, there is a reasonably strong relationship between how long a person's arms are and how long his or her legs are.

CHAPTER 7
HOW SCIENTISTS DISCUSS THEIR DATA

Scientists discuss their data in particular ways, especially when they write about it. Since students write lab reports about the investigations they do, it might be useful for them to know some of the ways scientists write about their findings in journal articles so they may use these approaches in their own writing.

USING HEDGING LANGUAGE WHEN INTERPRETING DATA

Making statements that indicate degrees of certainty is the normal practice in science writing. Although written claims in science are often probabilistic in this way, that does not mean that the scientist thinks there is doubt a relationship exists.

Research writing is directed to one's own writing community, so ideas can be evaluated and (one hopes) accepted by that community. Part of that evaluation and acceptance occurs because a scientist is very careful about stating how much of a relationship there is between the factors being studied. If a scientist overstates the relationship, others may not believe it, whereas if they understate a data relationship they may miss something that's going on. So, to make sure that they are accurately conveying the strength of a relationship, scientists use what's called hedging language. Hedging language is particularly characteristic of research writing that deals with new knowledge and new relationships.

In schools, student writing in science has traditionally been quite deterministic: "A causes B" or "dogs run faster than cats." Such deterministic language is problematic because it can influence how much evidence one expects is needed before science claims can be made. In addition, deterministic language states science findings in a very polarized way that does not well reflect the sorts of conclusions that scientists actually *do* draw.

Let's look at examples from each of the types of data we've discussed to see how you could write about the conclusions using hedging language (Figure 7.1).

FIGURE 7.1

Comparing sleep times for cats and dogs with nominal data

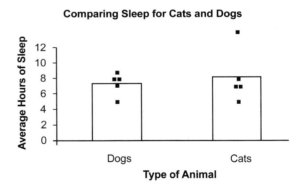

Nominal data—A "good" science conclusion: On average, it looks as if dogs sleep a bit less than cats. However, in the sample population, one cat slept a lot more than the other cats, and this might have affected the average for cats more than it should have (only a larger sample size would help us sort this out; maybe one in five cats does sleep a lot more than the other cats). Given the influence that one cat might have had on the overall average sleep for cats, it is possible that there is very little difference in the averages of how much cats and dogs sleep.

Note that the statement referred to the average, mentioned the possible influence of an obvious outlier, discussed the influence of sample size, and used terms like "bit," "it is possible," and "very little difference" to convey the *certainty* about relationships that were possible from this study. This represents a good use of hedging language to make appropriate claims about relationships.

Ordinal-level data has an extra step that makes it more complicated than interval-ratio data because there are now two factors that you look for when drawing conclusions. First, as with nominal data, you might well examine the graph for comparisons between individual factors. Second, you need to review it for trends across the graph in relation to what the ordinal-level data was illustrating as changing (the *x*-axis pattern, in other words).

In the following graph (Figure 7.2), we see the time it took for three different dog breeds to run between two points 30 m apart.

FIGURE 7.2

Comparing the speeds of different breeds of dogs with ordinal data

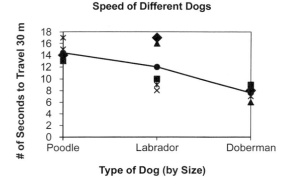

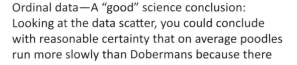

Ordinal data—A "good" science conclusion: Looking at the data scatter, you could conclude with reasonable certainty that on average poodles run more slowly than Dobermans because there

is almost no overlap in the data scatter for each of them. However, it is more difficult to draw conclusions from the data about the Labradors because the data scatter is so much greater than for either of the other two dog breeds. It is possible that Labradors could consistently run as fast as the Dobermans, but sometimes the Labradors run more slowly. Overall there seems to be somewhat of a pattern of bigger dogs running more quickly than smaller dogs, but the data scatter around the Labradors makes this conclusion a weak one, so it is not possible to draw this as a definitive conclusion. If notes about dog behavior had been taken during the data collection, it might have helped draw stronger conclusions.

Note that the statement referred to the average and to the influence of the data scatter around the Labrador data in drawing a conclusion; discussed the need for notes to be taken during data observation (to help explain the Labrador data); and used terms such as "reasonable certainty," "more difficult," and "somewhat of a pattern" to convey the certainty about relationships that were possible from this study. In addition, it mentioned the overall pattern that could be discerned ("bigger dogs seem to run more quickly than smaller dogs") but mentioned that it was a "weak conclusion" because of the scatter in the data for the Labradors.

Finally, let's look at a relationship in a causal but not a correlational graph depicting two measured variables (Figure 7.3).

FIGURE 7.3

Comparing arm- and leg-length data in teens with interval ratio data

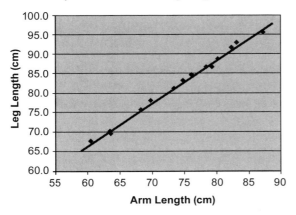

A Comparison of Arm and Leg Length in Teens

Interval-ratio data—A "good" science conclusion: According to the data in this study, there is a very strong relationship between arm length and leg length in teenagers because the data points are so close to the line of best fit. Overall, there is very little deviation of the data from the trend line, and there are no outliers in the data sample. This would be very useful information if you were making one-piece suits, such as floater suits for going out on boats, because you could make the arm length a very particular length in relation to the leg length and have it fit most teenagers.

This graph shows an example of a *very* strong relationship between two variables. The strength of this relationship is clearly conveyed by the use of the phrase "very strong" and is further emphasized by mentioning that there are no data points that lie away from the trend line that could be considered outliers. The strength of this relationship is made clear to the reader by describing a way in which this information could be used in the construction of floater suits.

TALKING ABOUT DATA IN RESEARCH INVESTIGATION REPORTS

Student laboratory reports are often premised on the assumption that the graph itself has meaning embedded in it. Consequently, there is often very little interpretation of the graph or data provided in those reports.

However, meaning doesn't exist in the graphs themselves, but rather lies in the interpretation. As a result, different people may interpret a graph somewhat differently, or even a lot differently, based on their interests and past experiences. Clearly, this could cause problems with someone reading reports that provide little or no description of how to interpret the graphs because they might draw different conclusions than the author(s) of the report intended.

How do scientists deal with this when they write their research reports?

It's pretty straightforward really. Scientists (1) have detailed captions explaining what the graphics are about and (2) provide detailed written interpretations of the graphs in the data section so that the reader reaches the same conclusions from the graphs that the authors themselves did. In professional science reports (in journals or at conferences), scientists seem to assume that the reader needs *everything* explained to them in almost excruciating detail—it's often almost as if they're assuming that the reader is incapable of interpreting the graphs or data tables for themselves. However, such an approach means that their work is not misinterpreted by another scientist and that it leads to convincing claims.

In general, what we're arguing is that students need to spend more time interpreting the graphs (and/or tables) and providing more detailed written interpretations in their laboratory reports of the patterns or trends they see. In addition, they need to work at providing more detailed captions (or titles) for the graphs and tables that they submit with assignments. Often we are struck by the lack of detail in the captions or titles on graphs and diagrams that are submitted by students in their laboratory reports.

Teaching Hint: Science reports are generally designed so that the science claims in the conclusion or discussion section are convincing. One could look at the literature review, the methodology section, the number of replicates, the data representations (graphs and tables), and the analysis of that data as all contributing to the "convincingness" of the final claims in the report. If the final claim(s) in a science reports are not convincing, then the author hasn't accomplished his or her goal(s). Basically, the reason scientists do all of their thinking, research, and writing is to achieve "convincingness." When encouraging our own students when they are doing science investigations, we often say, "I'm not convinced yet. How could you be more convincing?" as a way of encouraging them to do better work.

SUBSTANTIVE VERSUS STATISTICAL DIFFERENCE

There is a final distinction in reports that scientists sometimes make that we feel is important to mention, and that's the difference between a *significant* difference and a *substantive* difference.

A researcher might well conclude that the data are showing a significant difference (such as would be determined by a statistical test) between data means for instance, but that the difference itself is not substantive (or, in other words, important).

For instance, maybe Dobermans can run significantly faster than Labrador retrievers, but the difference is only a 2% difference over 30 m. Sure, it might be a statistically significant difference, but maybe it isn't a difference that matters in the real world. In that case, the research might discuss the difference as being significant but reasonably unimportant.

SECTION II
MORE ADVANCED WAYS OF COLLECTING, SHOWING, AND ANALYZING DATA

If you've made your way through the first section, or you have a beginning background in data analysis from your undergraduate degree, then this next section provides you with more complex ways of collecting and working with data.

WHAT

This section provides an introduction to the types of simple statistical analysis (including the calculations) that are most useful for determining whether the differences between means are statistically significant (in the previous section, we were learning to "eyeball" whether the differences were worth discussing). These tests include those for comparing pairs of means (the t-test), comparing many means (the analysis of variance [ANOVA] test), and understanding the relationship between two interval-ratio variables (regression analysis with correlation analysis).

In addition we provide an introduction to survey design and analysis. A common activity in both regular and science classes is collecting data using surveys (or questionnaires). Often these surveys are designed and analyzed without a proper foundation in how to do either task in a way that allows you to actually draw good conclusions. All too often in schools we have seen poorly designed surveys used to make decisions that the data didn't support. The relevant chapters in this section provide details and examples about how to design and interpret survey questions in a way that will lead to drawing better conclusions about what they mean—ways that will work either for your students or you.

WHO

We have seen students in grade 7 and up (admittedly advanced ones) do t-tests as part of analyzing inquiry science investigations (particularly for science fair projects). More advanced analysis, such as is discussed in this section, can be done by high school students as part of independent projects.

Simple surveys can be designed and used by students in primary grades as a way of teaching them how to collect data, show it in tables, summarize it with frequency counts, and show it in simple bar graphs. Middle school and upper grade students often design and use surveys as part of curricular units. We have also seen teachers design surveys for their classes so they can make decisions about their teaching.

These chapters aren't meant for teachers to copy and pass on to students (although the related resources in the appendixes can be), but they will help you understand the associated issues so you can then help your own students analyze data and design and analyze surveys.

HOW

Most of the parts of this section deal with more advanced material and would generally be used for enrichment activities, particularly for advanced students in middle school and high school. Information in all of these chapters is relevant for the independent investigation projects called for in some curricula.

CHAPTER 8
SIMPLE STATISTICS FOR SCIENCE TEACHERS: THE *t*-TEST, ANOVA TEST, AND REGRESSION AND CORRELATION COEFFICIENTS

In earlier chapters (Chapters 3 and 4), we looked at patterns in nominal data using bar graphs and ordinal data using line graphs. We "eyeballed" differences from those graphs, looking at the size of the circles drawn around the tics, and drew conclusions that we discussed using hedging language. But is that what scientists do?

Actually yes, in the early stages of their research or as the research is progressing—but it's not how they write their final reports. Those final reports often contain statistical analyses that allow the scientist to state with more certainty what differences and patterns they have found in their data. Remember what we mentioned earlier? That science was a probabilistic endeavor? Well, part of it being probabilistic is that scientists want to state with as much certainty as possible what the patterns and relationships are that they are looking at. Using statistics helps scientists improve the certainty of their statements so they can be as precise as possible.

In this chapter, we're going to look at three basic statistical tests. The first is the *t*-test, which is used when you have nominal or ordinal data and *only* two test variables you are comparing (e.g., the speed of cats and dogs). The second is the analysis of variance (ANOVA) test for when you have nominal or ordinal data and *more* than two test variables (e.g., the speed of cats and dogs and pigs). The third statistical analysis is correlation and regression analysis, which is for interval-ratio data when you are comparing two things you have measured (e.g., the amount of salt in the pot and how long it takes potatoes to cook). These three basic tests cover most of the types of inquiry studies we've seen grade 7–12 students conduct. There

are tests for more complicated designs, but this is a basic introduction, and understanding these will help you understand more complicated designs if you need to.

In a book like this, we should probably mention *why* this chapter is here. Statistical tests don't *seem* very basic do they? We agree that they're not; however, we've seen projects by grade 7 students (at science fairs) in which they used *t*-tests and could describe how the tests worked and why they used them. Correctly, we should add. We've seen ANOVA tests used by grade 10 students in the same settings, and by grade 12 students as part of inquiry investigations in their regular classes. As a teacher you never know when you're going to have that hyper-keen student in grade 8, so we thought you might appreciate having some resources to help you work with them. If nothing else, the worksheets we provide will give you something to give them to enhance their learning when they've raced ahead of the rest of the class. Besides that, this chapter might help you understand some of those mail-outs from boards of education with statistics in them that most of us have trouble making heads or tails of.

In Appendix IX we provide three resources: Worksheets that do a step-by-step calculation of each of these types of statistical analysis, critical value tables that let you determine if there are statistically significant differences, and a worked-through example for each test from data used in previous chapters in this book. We'll also mention that in the Resource section (Appendix VI) there are links to websites that also conduct these tests if you insert the data into them.[1] This chapter is an

---

1. We also intend to provide a resource page with analysis tools at the NSTA Press website for the book.

introductory description of what these tests are doing and the conditions that should be met for doing them.

THE *t*-TEST

The *t*-test is used when you compare *two* means to see if they are statistically different from each other. You should *not* use a *t*-test over and over to compare many pairs of means (see the ANOVA test description for how to deal with that situation). What the *t*-test is doing is determining what the likelihood is that the difference between the two means happens because of chance or because of the variable you tested. In simple terms, it's comparing how much data scatter there is for each variable and then comparing how different the means are in relation to that data scatter so that the likelihood of the differences between the means being due to random chance can be determined.

It might be a bit simpler if we looked at a graph of data (Figure 8.1 here, which you might recognize from Figure 1.7, p. 10).

A *t*-test would help you determine whether the amount of overlap in the data would be statistically significant so that you could argue that the two means are different from each other.[2]

Every test has conditions (also known as assumptions) that must be met for the results to be valid. If you meet those conditions, statistical tests are pretty good at letting you know whether there's a statistically significant difference between means, but if you violate those assumptions then the tests might not be accurate. Here are the assumptions that should be met to do the *t*-test:

FIGURE 8.1

Graph of temperature data with arrows depicting range of response and the gray area depicting where the data overlaps

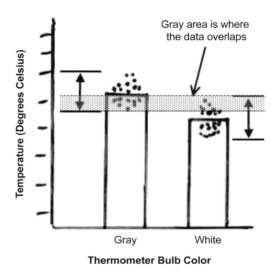

1. The data scatter is reasonably the same for the two categories (in statistical terms, the *variation* is close to the same).

2. There is more data toward the middle of the circles than at the nearest and farthest points away from the middle (in statistical terms, the data has a reasonably *normal distribution*).

3. The data are *randomly* chosen (in statistical terms, this means you didn't choose data to include so that you showed what you wanted to show).

4. The replicates in the two treatments need to be *independent* of each other. For instance, the data *cannot* be before and after measures on the same individuals (there's a separate test for that called the paired *t*-test).

---

2. We've actually done this in Appendix IX. Go and take a look at whether the means are significantly different or not for this data set.

It might be easier to show you what this means on a graph. Let's look at Figure 1.7 (the gray and white thermometer data, p. 10) again in Figure 8.2.

FIGURE 8.2

Depiction of gray and white temperature data portraying even data scatter

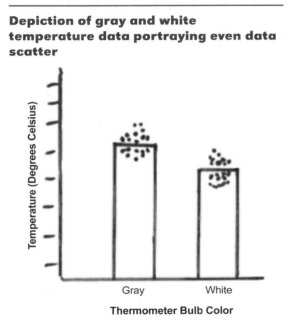

You'll notice that the data in this graph meets the assumptions listed above: The raw data depicted around the two bars is about the same distance from top to bottom, and there are more data points close to the horizontal line than far away from it.

Let's look at a couple of extreme versions of data for the same variables that do not meet those assumptions for a *t*-test (Figure 8.3).

FIGURE 8.3

Depiction of gray and white temperature data portraying uneven data scatter

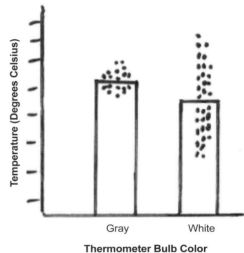

Notice that in Figure 8.3, the data on the right bar is much more scattered (has a greater variation) than the data on the left. This violates assumption 1. Now we'll look at a graph that violates assumption 2 (Figure 8.4, p. 54).

FIGURE 8.4

Depiction of gray and white temperature data portraying discontinuous data scatter

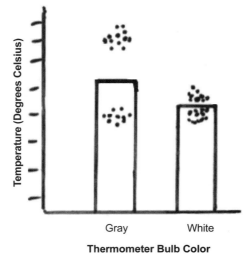

Thermometer Bulb Color

Here, you'll notice that on the left bar data are not close to the horizontal line at all; the horizontal line is at the average of two separate clusters. This condition violates assumption 2 because the data are not normally distributed (i.e., more toward the horizontal line than away from it).

The more your data looks like the last two graphs (and data could look like a combination of both of them), the less likely it is that the results of the t-test are reliable. In that situation you might *hedge* how you phrased your interpretation of the data analysis. For instance, if you found a significant difference (as we will describe below), you could write, "Despite finding a significant difference between the mean temperatures for the gray and white thermometer, there is still some room for doubt because of the amount of variation in the data for the white thermometer, which was much greater than that for the gray thermometer."

However, having described the problem, realize that the t-test is a reasonably robust test and is fairly accurate even if its assumptions are violated.

So, how do you calculate a t-test? The step-by-step worksheet and example in Appendix IX will show you. When you calculate your t-test statistic using the worksheet, compare your calculated value to the table value in Table 8.1.

TABLE 8.1

Critical values for the t-test statistic

5% Significance Table			
Degrees of freedom	Critical value	Degrees of freedom	Critical value
4	2.78	15	2.13
5	2.57	16	2.12
6	2.48	18	2.10
7	2.37	20	2.09
8	2.31	22	2.07
9	2.26	24	2.06
10	2.23	26	2.06
11	2.20	28	2.05
12	2.18	30	2.04
13	2.16	40	2.02
14	2.15	60	2.00
		120	1.98

If the t-statistic you calculated is *less than* the critical value in the table above (for the correct degrees of freedom, which you calculate on the worksheet) then the difference between the two means is not statistically significant.

If the calculated *t*-statistic is *greater than* the critical value in the table above (for the correct degrees of freedom) then the difference between the two means is statistically significant at 5%. This means we're 95% confident that the difference between the means is a real one (i.e., not due to chance).

THE ANOVA TEST

The ANOVA test is used when you have several different treatments you are testing (in other words, more than two treatments). Sometimes people do multiple *t*-tests instead of an ANOVA—this is *bad, bad, bad*. Very bad. Ghostbusters bad. Why? Because you considerably increase the likelihood that you'll report a statistically significant difference when there is *not* one. All of those "only 1 in 20 chances of being wrong" possibilities add up so it becomes *very* likely that you're wrong. An ANOVA test stops that from happening.

Note that the treatments have to be either nominal- or ordinal-category-type data categories, treatments, or groups, and you have to have collected measured data about them.

If, for instance, you measured how fast three different breeds of dogs (with increasing sizes) could run 30 m, then that would be the type of data you would do an ANOVA test on. You have ordinal categories, and you have the times it took to cover the distance.

But why would you?

You can *see* the differences in the graph can't you?

Well, an ANOVA test allows you to figure out if the differences between the mean times to run 30 m are different enough, given the way the data are scattered about the mean, to say *with certainty* that the breeds of dogs can run at different speeds. It might seem a bit odd to "test" this, because you can *see* that the means look different on a graph, but scientists care about how much data scatter there is too, which is why these statistical tests were created! And doing an ANOVA test allows you to be more convincing when making arguments about your findings to others (that's why scientists do statistical analyses: They remove some of the personal bias that might influence their interpretations, so they become more convincing with their claims).

First, it's important to note that the ANOVA test has some conditions that must be met (just as the *t*-test did; in fact, they're basically the same conditions, so you can look at the graphical examples from the *t*-test if you need to). Here are the conditions that must be met to perform an ANOVA test:

1. The data scatter is reasonably the same for the two categories (in statistical terms, the *variation* is close to the same).

2. There is more data scatter toward the middle of the circles than at the nearest and farthest points away from the middle (in statistical terms, the data has a reasonably *normal distribution*).

3. The data are *randomly* chosen (in statistical terms this means you didn't choose only data to include so that you showed only what you wanted to show).

4. The replicates in the treatments need to be *independent* of each other (one treatment cannot be influencing another).

We've been using the phrase *data scatter* to discuss how the raw data spreads out around the mean, but the more correct term is *variance*. So, an ANOVA test really is—ready for it?—an ANalysis Of VAriance. An ANOVA test analyzes the variance around each of the means and the overall variance to figure out how certain you can be about whether the means are different from each other.

Okay, so let's say that we've collected data looking at how fast the three different dog breeds can run a 30 m distance, and we've tested five different dogs of each breed (Table 8.2).

That data would give us a graph that looks like Figure 8.5.

TABLE 8.2

Time in seconds that different dog breeds can run 30 m

Dog	Poodle	Labrador	Doberman
1	14	17	8
2	13	10	9
3	13	16	6
4	15	8	8
5	17	9	7
Avg.	14.4 s	12 s	7.6 s

FIGURE 8.5

The time it takes different dog breeds to run 30 m, ordered by dog size

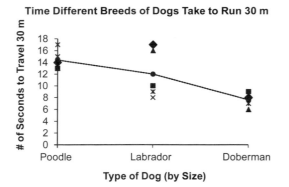

Notice that this graph looks a little bit different from those you might get from a

spreadsheet. That's because all of the data are on it, not just the average of the times each breed ran 30 m. Because you can see the data scatter around each average (at the dot where the line is), you can get a bit of an idea about what an ANOVA test does. Basically, it compares the data scatter around each mean *and* the overall data scatter *and* where each mean is and figures out if the means are different from each other. Essentially, the ANOVA test is analyzing how much the data you see on the graph overlap *in relation to the total amount of data scatter*. If the data do not overlap enough, then the means are probably different from each other. If they overlap a lot, in relation to the total amount of data scatter, then the means probably are *not* different from each other. The graph in Figure 8.6 might help you picture this.

FIGURE 8.6

The time it takes different breeds of dogs to run 30, ordered by dog size with an arrow depicting the overall range of response and the gray area depicting where the data overlaps for the pairs of variables

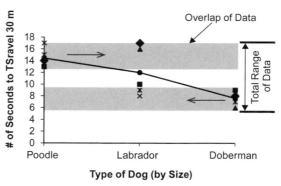

As with the *t*-test, the ANOVA test is a pretty robust test, and this means that the variation in the data scatter around the mean can be a bit off (as it is with the Labrador) and the test will still be valid.

However, it gets a bit more complicated drawing conclusions from the ANOVA test compared to the *t*-test. In the *t*-test, there was only one pair of data, and we knew that the significant difference was just between that pair. But in the ANOVA, if the means are found to be statistically significant from each other overall, we still don't know *which* means were statistically significant from each other; we *cannot* assume that they all were. In this dog study, for instance, we know that there is a statistical difference between means (see Appendix IX for a worked-out example) but not whether Dobermans are faster than poodles, Labradors are faster than poodles, or Dobermans are faster than Labradors (the three possible pair comparisons).

There are tests, called *post hoc* (meaning after) tests, which can be done for this, but they're complicated enough that we're not going to include them here.[3]

That does not, however, mean that you cannot draw conclusions—we can look at the graph. The *first* important point is this: if you do an ANOVA test and do not find a statistically significant result for the whole data set, then it does *not* matter what the graph looks like—how far apart the means are—because there *is no statistically significant difference,* and that result means a whole lot more than any eyeballing differences. We're emphasizing this point because even undergraduates in science have difficulty understanding this. No statistical significance means, wait for it, waaiiittt for it … no statistical significance … no difference between means. Just what it says. Okay? None.

But what if you *do* find statistical significance for the whole data set after doing an ANOVA test? Well, then looking at the graph to help figure out the paired means is completely valid.

Let's look at our data in Figure 8.5 again. How would we analyze it? Let's assume that our ANOVA was significant. Now we have to figure out the differences between pairs of data. We should probably look at the amount of overlap.

When you do this, you note that the lack of overlap of the two gray areas (one drawn across covering the poodle data, the other drawn across covering the Doberman data) *probably* means that the average times of poodles and Dobermans are significantly different from each other. (Note the use of hedging language in that statement? Also note that we haven't used the word *statistically* because we don't know about that specific pair statistically since we haven't run a statistical test.) However, there was so much variation in the Labrador data that it's difficult to draw any strong conclusions about the differences in the mean times of the different breeds. The average times for the Labradors and the Dobermans were pretty far from each other, and the time data of each breed only overlapped a little, so the mean times are quite possibly different from each other (so, significantly different from each other). However, the time data for the poodles and the Labradors overlapped enough that it's possible that the means for those breeds are *not* different from each other—or in other words, that there is no difference between the means for the poodle and the Labrador dogs. So, from an inspection of the data scatter on the graph it would be safe to conclude that

- poodles are *very probably* slower than Dobermans;

---

3. A common post-hoc test for dog data such as in the example is called Tukey's test.

- Dobermans are *possibly* faster than Labradors; and

- poodles *might be* the same speed as Labradors.

Without statistical testing this is a qualitative determination and therefore hedging language is used for all of the pair comparisons.[4]

Again, with an ANOVA analysis these differences would have a percentage certainty, or likelihood of error, associated with them just like the *t*-test, and in the tables provided with the worksheets (see Appendix IX) there is a 95% certainty in your answer (of statistical significance of differences in the entire data set), or a 5% possibility of error rate.

CORRELATION AND REGRESSION ANALYSIS

This type of data analysis is done on interval-ratio measures for which you want to find out if one factor (or variable) changes when another one does. Basically, when you have a graph of data, the regression analysis (or line of best fit analysis) is determining what the best average line is through the data set, and the correlation coefficient analysis is a measure of just how good that average is (i.e., how much the data are scattered about that line). This calculation is *not* a significance test (as the *t*-test and ANOVA test were), so you're not determining whether the slope of the line of best fit is significantly different from something else.

A correlation coefficient is a calculated statistic representing how close the data points are to the line of best fit. If you multiply the correlation coefficient by itself (see the

worksheet in Appendix IX), then you obtain a value that tells you the percentage of variation in variable *y* as explained by variable *x* (in a *causal* relationship). The closer this value is to 1 (or 100%, since you often multiply the product by 100), then the closer the values are to the line. In Figure 8.7 (a–c), you see three lines of best fit with different amounts of data scatter around them.

FIGURE 8.7

Examples of different types of scatterplot relationships

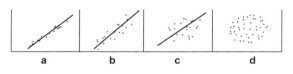

a   b   c   d

In this example, (a) would have an *r*-squared value close to 100%. At the other extreme, (d), any plotted line of best fit would have an *r*-squared value close to 0% (in other words, there is no relationship between the two variables). There are no hard and fast rules in science as to how much of an *r*-squared value is needed to talk about relationships between the variables. It can vary quite considerably depending on the circumstances. However, the *r*-squared value *does* give you guidance as to how you should be using hedging language to talk about the relationship between the variables.

Remember, in Appendix IX we provide worksheets for doing *t*-tests and ANOVA tests as well as worked-through examples. Appendix VIII also demonstrates a *t*-test analysis.

As a conclusion to this chapter we are going to provide an example of a correlation analysis in the form of a case study. In this case study, you'll find a student report on an investigation and then a teacher's feedback on that report.

_____

4. A Tukey's test at 5% indicates that there is a significant difference between the poodle and Doberman means, but *no difference* between the poodle-Labrador *or* Labrador-Doberman mean times. This reflects the broad scatter in the Labrador times.

CASE STUDY: STUDENT REGRESSION AND CORRELATION ANALYSIS WITH TEACHER COMMENTARY

STUDENT RESEARCH QUESTION: DOES MY GUINEA PIG SLEEP MORE WHEN IT EATS MORE?

METHOD

1. Put 100 g of pellet food in my guinea pig's bowl each day.

2. Each morning replace the food bowl with a new one with 100 g of pellet food, pick up any pellets lying around and put them in the old food bowl, and weigh the old food bowl. Subtract the total remaining food from 100 g to get how much my guinea pig has eaten. Record the data in the data table.

3. Use a video camera with a time counter attached to my computer to record the amount of time my guinea pig sleeps in its box (I used a special camera with an infrared light that could see my guinea pig in the dark). Each day, fast-forward through the recording and keep track of how many minutes the guinea pig lies down with its eye facing the camera (mostly) closed (What looks like sleep … most sleep with their eyes open, mine usually doesn't). Record the number of minutes in the data table (Table 8.3).

4. Keep hay and water in the cage so that there is always some. The only food being tracked is the pellets.

5. Do steps 2–4 for 30 days.

TABLE 8.3

A student's data on how much guinea pigs sleep in relation to how much they eat

Day	Pellets eaten (g)	Sleep in 24 h (min)
1	38	185
2	40	220
3	48	217
4	42	260
5	41	270
6	47	235
7	50	195
8	43	270
9	45	269
10	49	258
11	53	310
12	45	420
13	31	350
14	50	310
15	42	210
16	53	270
17	54	304
18	51	331
19	60	321
20	61	215
21	62	265
22	55	254
23	65	300
24	61	325
25	60	335
26	60	355
27	68	355
28	80	435
29	58	357
30	70	330

Because I had *x-y* data, I graphed it in a scatterplot so that I could see any pattern better (Figure 8.8).

FIGURE 8.8

A scatterplot of the data shown in Table 8.3, p. 59

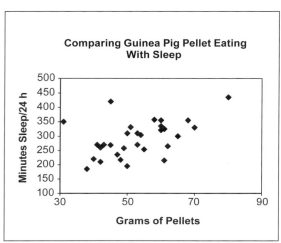

I also calculated the regression formula and correlation coefficient using the worksheets you gave us, so I knew how good my calculated line of best fit represented the data.

Regression formula: $y = 2.7x + 145$

Correlation coefficient: 0.23 or 23%

CONCLUSION

I only have one guinea pig, so I can't say anything about all guinea pigs, but I can say that when mine eats more it seems to sleep longer, at least reasonably often. The correlation coefficient is only 23%, which means that the line doesn't fit the data really well, but those two high amounts of sleep on the top left of the graph might have made it weaker. Maybe I should calculate the regression line and the correlation coefficient without them because when I draw the line on the graph from the regression formula the line seems kind of high. I would do the study with more guinea pigs if I had them because maybe my pig isn't normal and doesn't sleep in the same way as others.

INSTRUCTOR FEEDBACK TO STUDENT

You did a good job studying your guinea pig and figuring out the relationship between the amount of food and the amount of sleep. You wrote about it really well. You described how strong the relationship is (shown by your correlation coefficient) quite effectively by using the hedging language we've talked about in class. You're right, the relationship between the pellet consumption and the amount of sleep each day isn't a strong one (as indicated by the 23% value), but it is there. We haven't talked about this in class, but in physics that number might be really low, but when you're describing animal behaviour and many other things, a 23% correlation is actually really good. It means you're predicting 23% of what an animal is doing. I also think you're right by the way, if you excluded those two values on the top left of your page (who knows why your pig slept longer on those days—maybe it ate more hay than normal, or maybe it ran on its wheel more than it normally does) then your correlation would be *much* higher. When I exclude them and calculate your correlation coefficient it jumps up to 53%, and for animal behaviour that is really high.

I have a question for you: Why are you sure that it is the pellet consumption that is causing the amount of sleep? We did talk about the difference between *correlation* and *causation* in class. On the one hand, it does seem reasonable. I'm always sleepy after a big dinner. On the other hand, something else is also going on that might affect how the guinea pig behaves. Winter is coming, right? What else happens then? I bet if you think about it you'll remember that when winter comes it's darker for a longer time—the daytime is shorter. What effect might less daylight have on the amount of sleep a guinea pig would want to get? Do they have alarm clocks? What do you think wakes them up? So how would we look at this? If it were the length of the day, you'd think your pig would eat more later in your study than earlier *and* would sleep more later in your study than at the beginning. Let's graph this (Figure 8.9).

So, do you see that? The food consumption goes up over the 30 days of your study and the sleep *also* goes up over those 30 days. So maybe the amount of daylight is affecting both how much your pig sleeps and how much it eats. This probably means that the amount of pellets consumed is *correlated* with the amount of sleep, but *not* the *cause* of the amount of sleep. Other than missing that (which even I admit was pretty tricky), your study and your report were both well done.

If you want to test whether it was daylight that had an effect, you could do your study again in the spring when the length of daylight is getting longer and see if there was a decrease in the amount of time your guinea pig slept. Let me know what you find out.

FIGURE 8.9

The teacher's graphs compare sleep and food consumption over a number of days

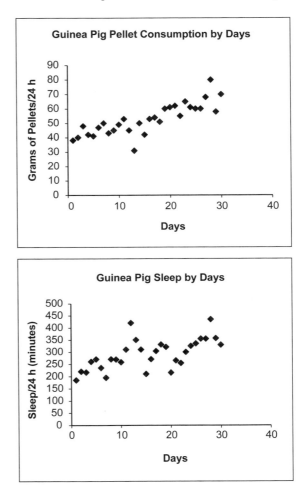

CHAPTER 9
DOING SURVEYS WITH KIDS: ASKING GOOD QUESTIONS, MAKING SENSE OF ANSWERS

This might seem like an odd chapter to put in a book on the basics of data literacy, but during our visits to schools and in our classes we find more and more teachers talking about having their students conduct surveys or questionnaires. From a data literacy perspective, we decided to include chapters on this topic because the research questions in questionnaires are different from those people generally learn to ask in science. Additionally, the data is a different type from that which is normally learned about in science programs, and it needs to be analyzed in a way that is different from the way science students normally learn to analyze data (including the ways we've shown you in previous chapters).

As far as we can tell, teachers have their students work on questionnaires (1) to help them connect the science they are learning about in classrooms to actions or decisions made by the public (either their peers or adults) and/or (2) to help them make comparisons between what the public knows about an issue and what they themselves know. Sometimes the questions deal with attitudes toward socioscientific issues such as conservation of electricity, recycling, or climate change. At other times, questions are along the lines of "Do you know as much about issue X as a seventh grader?"

Let's take a look at some questions typically found in a student survey (in this case about recycling).

> When was the last time you drank a soda that came in a plastic bottle?
>
> _____

> Did you recycle that plastic bottle?
> ____ Yes ____ No

> Do you usually recycle plastic bottles? ____Yes ____ No

These questions seem pretty straightforward, but are there better ways of asking them? that give you better insights? ways that allow you to get more details so that you can do a better analysis of the results? The answer to all of these questions is, of course, yes. These questions, by the way, represent the two basic types of questions: *open-ended* (for which you can provide any answer you choose) and *closed-ended* (for which you're choosing from options provided by those who designed the survey).

So, we won't go into details about the need for proper spelling and clear grammar and punctuation—teachers keep an eye out for those sorts of things anyway. But what we will do is go over some basic question types (there are others, of course) and provide examples of questions from a good and a bad design perspective. We will summarize important points as Question Design Rules throughout the chapter.

First, however, we should probably list the steps to designing a questionnaire or survey.

1. Figure out what you want to know about. You might have to break bigger questions into smaller parts.

2. Determine what your questionnaire will be like. Will you hand it out for people to fill out themselves? Will you ask them questions verbally and fill it out for them? Will you do it online

(using a tool such as Surveymonkey. com) and e-mail it to them?

3. Determine the question content that will give you the information you want.

4. Figure out what kind of response you want for the question.

5. Work on the exact wording.

6. Put the questions into an effective sequence (demographic information usually goes at the front or the back).

7. Test the questionnaire and revise it. Repeat this one or two times.

8. Conduct your questionnaire (handout, e-mail, etc.).

9. Analyze your responses.

There are five general types of questions found on surveys (and many variants of those; we provide a list of them so you can look them up) that we are going to discuss in this chapter.

FIVE GENERAL TYPES OF QUESTIONS

YES/NO QUESTIONS (OR "TWO DISCRETE CATEGORIES" QUESTIONS)

Students ask these sorts of questions to help find out absolute sorts of answers (and it is easy to see how they might derive from the deterministic versus probabilistic approaches to science relationships often present in school science, as we argued earlier).

> *Question Design Rule #1:* Try to make your phrasing as clear as possible. You must examine each question in your questionnaire in great detail so that you are sure the reader will understand the question in the way intended by the person who wrote the question.

If we look at the question, "Do you usually recycle plastic bottles?" you can see that if you think critically about it that interpreting the question hinges on the reader's interpretation of the word *usually*. For some respondents the word *usually* will mean 50% or more of the time, and for other respondents it will mean 90% or more of the time. Even more confusingly, *usually* for some respondents could also mean whenever recycling is available. This sort of flexibility in interpreting words makes the question answers very difficult to interpret.

> *Question Design Rule #2*: Yes/No questions should deal with situations in which there are absolutes, in which there is no possibility of another answer.

Can we make this question a bit better? Yes, the phrasing "Do you recycle plastic bottles most of the time?" might give a better indication of how often the person recycles plastic bottles, but although the word *most* is a bit more specific than *usually*, there might still be interpretation problems (by the respondent and in the analysis). Better yet is the question, "Do you recycle plastic bottles more than 30% of the time?" because it is even clearer.

The job of someone writing a survey question is to try and anticipate the different ways someone might respond to a survey and to take those possible responses into account in the phrasing of the question. It is quite difficult to be perfect, but trying to make the phrasing as clear as possible is a necessary part of designing a survey so that the results are interpretable. You need to make sure that the answers to the question indicate as clearly as possible to the person who designed the questionnaire what the person replying meant. In this example, "Do you usually recycle plastic bottles?" because of the flexibility understanding what the reader might take the word *usually* to mean, it is difficult to interpret either the "yes" or the "no" response. So how can this be dealt with? The answer is that this may not be a good type of thing to find out about using a Yes/No format of question (what if they did it 32% of the time? that's pretty close isn't it?). A different format of question might provide better insights (we will give examples of these later).

So what type of question might be a better sort of question for the Yes/No format?

How about the question
Answer Yes/No to the following:

> A. Do you own a cat? _____ Does the cat live in your house? _____

or

> B. Do any cats live in the household(s) where you live? _____

The phrasing in (B) solves the problem in the (A) question with owning cats (because a roommate or tenant might own them), or the use of the word *house* (when the respondent lives in an apartment) or that the student splits living with mom and dad (using the plural). When you're designing surveys (or critiquing those of your students) you need to *make sure the questions are as specific as possible*.

> Question Design Rule #3: Any type of data (which here we are calling frequency data) for which the question is checked or not checked *should not* be analyzed using a *t*-test or an ANOVA test. You also should not calculate arithmetic averages with the data.

As a final comment, although this question format was presented in Yes/No format questions, it is really about having two discrete categories for the answer, which means you must choose one *or* the other. Another question of this type could have Male or Female as possible answers. The distinction here is that (1) the response can be written with a "Yes" or "No," or (2) a check option can be used, e.g., _____M _____F (check off the appropriate box). In books on survey research, they refer to these as *dichotomous questions*. Note that the available options to dichotomous questions should include all responses that are actually possible.

YES/NO QUESTIONS: ANALYSIS

These questions are analyzed by counting responses; they are a *frequency data*[1] sort of question (as is the next sort of question). So, for instance, you could count the number of "yes" responses and the number of "no" responses and show them in a bar graph (as in Chapter 3). It is important to note that this type of data *should not* be analyzed using a *t*-test. Techniques are shown in the next chapter if you wanted to compare the answers to this question with the answers to another question.

---

1. In this chapter we make a distinction between *frequency data* questions in which the people answering the survey provide a checkbox, Yes/No, or other categorical answers that the researcher summarizes as frequencies, and *frequency estimates* which are estimates of frequencies (or percentages) provided by the people answering the survey.

COUNT QUESTIONS (INCLUDING "MANY DISCRETE CATEGORIES" QUESTIONS)

Count questions ask the person answering the questionnaire "how often?" or "how many?" and come in two types. The first type is open-ended: The respondent provides an interval-ratio number (which is usually discrete [which means they are usually whole-number responses]) in which they are providing an estimate[2] of, usually, some practice or experience. In other words, the questionnaire respondent is doing the counting. The second type is closed-ended, in which respondents choose from many discrete categories[3] provided by the questionnaire designer. In this type of count question, the person analyzing the survey counts the responses submitted by the respondents.

Say you were interested in how often people recycled plastic bottles of soda or water. You could ask

A. How many plastic bottles[4] of water or soda did you drink in the last seven days? _____

or

B. How many plastic bottles of water or soda did you drink in the last seven days? (please ∨)

____ none ____ (1–5) ____ (6–10)
____ (11–15) ____ (more than 15)

---

2. We refer to this as frequency estimate data, because the estimate of frequencies is provided by the questionnaire respondent.

3. Books on survey research refer to these as multichotomous questions.

4. If you wish to be really precise, you should probably include the phrase "individual serving" before "plastic bottles" to exclude the large-volume types of plastic bottles. Additionally, you might want to add "all or part of" after the word "drink" so that people are dealing with the numbers of bottles they opened. So, a really, really good question might be "How many individually-sized plastic bottles of water or soda did you drink all or part of in the last seven days?"

Clearly (A) is a higher-order sort of question because it deals with an interval-ratio value. On the other hand, (B) is a slightly lower-order question because it is dealing with increasing categories (and so is an ordinal-level question) and frequencies of responses of those broader categories. Common sense might suggest that you should always ask a higher-order question because you get more information from it, but should you? In this case, people answering the survey might skip the question because it's too much work for some people to remember exactly, or count back, how many bottles they drank in the last seven days. They were likely not keeping track as they went along. Most people could remember about how many, but exact numbers are more difficult, and people don't like putting "wrong" answers down on something that looks like a test, so they might put down nothing. It might be a better choice to offer them ranges, as in (B), so that they feel less stressed answering the question. Note, also, that in the category responses (in [B]), all possibilities of response are covered—there is no number of bottles they could have consumed that couldn't be accommodated in the range of possible responses.

> *Question Design Rule #4:* The more stressed or pressured someone answering a questionnaire feels by a question, the more likely they are to skip answering it. You get more information when you design a question that makes it easier for the people who are answering it.

COUNT QUESTIONS: ANALYSIS

Each of these two types offers some advantages from an analysis perspective. The responses to the first question, (A), are interval-ratio data, and you can simply do an arithmetic average on those results. Then you could compare the results between other question categories. Say you were interested in comparing the frequency of recycling by boys and girls: You could calculate an arithmetic average for each of those two categories and compare them using a bar graph (as in Chapter 3). Because the response is interval-ratio data, you could also do a *t*-test (Chapter 8) to statistically compare the tendencies for recycling between male and female students.

> *Question Design Rule #5:* Any question for which you are "counting" responses (i.e., determining a frequency of responses) cannot be analyzed using a *t*-test or an ANOVA test because they are counts not measures. There are statistical analyses for this type of data, such as the chi-square analysis, but they are not covered in this book.

For questions that are of the (B) type, you can calculate frequencies and show them in a bar graph (much as you could with the Yes/No question types) or if the data are ordinal (i.e., categorical and increasing but not in a consistent pattern), you might choose to use a line graph (as demonstrated in Chapter 4), although in this type of question line graphs are less common. Generally, *percentages* are reported for this sort of response (with the number of instances reported as $n = \#$ in the descriptive text in which the data are discussed), although for younger students raw counts would also be acceptable.

There is a variation on this type of question in which the (B) type is *not* ordinal. For instance, you could ask

> A. How many t-shirts do you own in each color?
>
> ____white ____black ____blue
> ____yellow ____pink ____green
> ____mixed ____other

or

> B. Place a checkmark (√) if you own any t-shirts in these colors:
>
> ____white ____black ____blue
> ____yellow ____pink ____green
> ____mixed ____other

Notice that in this instance the variable "t-shirt color" is not an ordinal variable but a nominal variable—there are just many categories of it.

In this case, the analysis would most likely not use a line graph to show the frequencies but would instead use a bar graph showing number of "yes" responses versus t-shirt color (or percentage, depending on the age of the students doing the questionnaire).

TABLE QUESTIONS

When designing a questionnaire, the appearance is often quite important: the nicer it looks, the more likely people will spend time answering it. Another factor is that it cannot look too long. This can be a real challenge if you want some detailed information; however, if you ask the questions concisely in a structured format, you can obtain the same information while having a *smaller-looking* survey (remember, the key is how the questionnaire looks). So, how can we do this? Using a table to collect responses can be helpful.

What if you wanted to know lots of information about pets using a small amount of space? You could create a chart like the one in Figure 9.1.

FIGURE 9.1

A potential survey table about pets
Please tell us about the pets you live with

	# of adults	# of young ones	# that are babies	Your pet (check of yes)	Your parent's pet (check if yes)	Your roommate or tenant's pet (check if yes)
Cats						
Dogs						
Rodents						
Rabbits						
Snakes						
Birds						
Other						

Notice that this question combines the different question types in the previous two categories (so the analysis would be the same), but rather than writing each question out, they're all combined efficiently in this table. Making your questions use space more efficiently can improve the responses you get (both in the questionnaire and *of* the questionnaire).

Analysis of these questions can be quite complex (because there is so much information), and you'll often have to refocus your students on exactly what they want to know. It helps if they're really clear about what they want to know about "in the big picture" before they have people fill out their questionnaire.

LIKERT/ATTITUDE ITEMS

Likert questions quite simply ask someone how much they agree or disagree with a statement (they are a variant of the many discrete category question type discussed above). This is often the most common type of question in a survey. Likert questions are usually finding out someone's opinion, attitude, or position on a topic. The actual items are not questions, they are statements, and the respondent indicates to what extent they agree or disagree with the statement.

> *Question Design Rule #6:* Remember the BFCs of question design. Keep your questions Brief, Focused, and Clear. This will lead to answers that better reflect what you actually want to know about and will increase your response rate.

The following is an example of a Likert item:

Please indicate the extent to which you agree with the statement "I think cats are the best pets."

1 = Strongly agree

2 = Agree

3 = Disagree

4 = Strongly disagree

There are several notable things about this example.

- First, they are not necessarily "reversible." Marking a (4) does not, in this case, indicate that you think that cats are the worst pets. If you want to find out the reverse of this question, you have to have a statement of the reverse: "I think cats are the worst pets."[5]

- Second, this question does not have a "neutral" or "no opinion" category. You could add one either as a middle option or as a fifth option. If you want to force an answer from the person so that they are indicating either a positive or negative response, then you do not use a middle or neutral category. Whether you do so or not in a question is a judgment call depending on what kind of response you are looking for.

- Third, and this is important (it is what we see done incorrectly most often in reporting survey results), you *cannot* arithmetically average the responses from the respondents; the responses are ordinal-level responses not interval-ratio responses (this also means that you *cannot* conduct a *t*-test or ANOVA test on the responses). The numbers 1 to 4 in that list could have just as easily been A to D, and you would never think of arithmetically averaging letters would you? Of course not. The only type of average that you can do with this data is a calculation of the *median* (or middle value when you place all responses in order). Otherwise, and this is what is normally done, you could report on the frequency of responses to each answer type and report these in a bar graph. (A more complex analysis, allowing you to compare responses on one question to those on another question, the frequency

data equivalent to a scatterplot, is described in the next chapter).

In the Likert example on the previous page, there are four possible responses, but other ranges are possible. In Table 9.1 (p. 70) we show the typical sorts of responses for two to seven item tests (although often in the survey only the end points are indicated).

It is most normal for surveys to have five choices, although surveys with four, six, or seven choices are also found. It is uncommon to find fewer than four or more than seven choices.

Sometimes researchers design Likert-scale questions after doing a *pilot study* in which they do interviews with test subjects about the issues they are interested in. For instance, if short pilot interviews with people were done to find out about how much they like dogs as pets, and that pilot study found out that dog size was an important factor, it might make more sense to ask three Likert questions about dogs as pets that included a reference to size. For instance, rather than getting people to state the degree to which they agree or disagree with the statement "I think dogs are the best pets," it instead might have to be broken down into three questions:

I think big dogs are the best pets.

I think medium-sized dogs are the best pets.

I think small dogs are the best pets.

And the respondents indicate how much they agree with each of the three statements.

---

5. One solution to this would be to use a different question type where "Cats as pets" was indicated on a multipoint scale running from "best pet" to "worst pet." This suggested question is a type of semantic differential scale (see below).

TABLE 9.1

Possible answers for Likert questions with different numbers of categories

Two categories						
		Disagree		Agree		
Three categories						
		Disagree	Neutral	Agree		
Four categories						
	Strongly disagree	Disagree		Agree	Strongly agree	
Five categories						
	Strongly disagree	Disagree	Neutral	Agree	Strongly agree	
Six categories						
Strongly disagree	Disagree	Slightly disagree		Slightly agree	Agree	Strongly agree
Seven categories						
Strongly disagree	Disagree	Slightly disagree	Neutral	Slightly agree	Agree	Strongly agree

One final point, often Likert-scale questions are clustered around bigger ideas so that people are being asked to indicate the degree to which they agreed or disagreed to a series of related statements on a bigger topic (for instance, questions that explored different statements about garbage and recycling and reduced consumption so that the analysis could get a broad understanding of the topic of pollution).

OPEN-ENDED WRITTEN RESPONSES

All of us have written this type of question—it's very much like an open-ended short-answer or essay question. "Discuss whether you think bullies should be expelled from school," and "If your parent(s) works, describe what they do when they get home from work," are two reasonable examples of this form of question. When designing the question, you should give clear instructions. You can tell the respondents to list things, describe in point form, argue for and against, and so on. You also have considerable control over the answers based on the amount of space you provide respondents for an answer. One issue with this type of question is that they can take a long time for someone to respond, so questionnaires often limit themselves to only one or two questions of this type.

OTHER QUESTION TYPES

So far we have covered the major types of questions found in simple surveys, but there are many other types of questions that can provide interesting information for analysis. There is no reason not to use them, but to look them up online to learn how to use them you have to know they exist, so we've provided a list of other survey questions below:

- the verbal frequency scale (similar to a Likert scale except dealing with frequency indicators)
- the ordinal scale (similar to a Likert scale except indicating one choice of an ordered outcome that isn't about degree of agreement)
- the forced ranking scale (ranking items provided in a list)
- the paired-comparison scale (choosing one of two paired options)
- the comparative scale (similar to a Likert scale except indicating one choice of strengths of comparison of one thing to another)
- the adjective checklist (choosing from a list of adjectives that relate to or describe something)
- the semantic differential scale (choosing the strength of how much a list of *paired* adjectives relate to or describe something)
- the Stapel scale (indicating numerically to what degree a list of adjectives describe or relate to something)
- the fixed sum scale (indicating numerically how often/much/etc. a list of things occurred)

- the graphical rating scale (a more-or-less visual approach to a Likert scale)
- a nonverbal or idiographic scale (more or less an iconic approach to a Likert scale)

We will, however, point out that with the five example question types we provided, you can construct a pretty comprehensive survey.

PROBLEMS THAT ARISE IN ASKING SURVEY QUESTIONS

Asking good survey questions is a skill that can take time to develop. Several types of errors that arise in survey questions can result in data that cannot be analyzed (at least to provide the insights one was hoping for). In this next section, we discuss several of the more common problems that come up in survey questions we've seen. After you have constructed your survey, you should go through these one at a time, comparing each described problem to the question being asked to make sure the survey question can be used.

THE OLD DOUBLE-BARRELED QUESTION: PROBLEMS WITH PARALLELISM

A double-barreled question tries to figure out too much at once. Think of the question,

> What types of pets do you own, and how long have you owned them?

The open-ended answer, "I have a dog and a snake and I've owned them four years and one year" *might* seem clear to us, but the problem is that respondents might not be listing the times in the same order as the pets. You *cannot* assume they are in the same order.

THE OLD DOUBLE-BARRELED QUESTION: PROBLEMS WITH DUAL ANSWERS

When you ask this sort of question, it is very difficult to interpret the data to understand what the question means. For instance, if you asked the question

> Do you think highway speeds should be lowered for cars and trucks?

You've really asked *two* questions. Think about it: Does a "yes" mean *both* cars and trucks or one but not the other? Does a "no" mean it has to be lowered for both? Or for one or the other?

Even worse, imagine if the respondent is stuck with answering because they want it lowered for trucks but not for cars. In those situations, the respondent might leave the question blank—and you've learned nothing even though they *do* have an opinion. It is far better to ask questions such as this as *two* distinct questions with *two* places to answer (one for each).

LACK OF FOCUS IN THE QUESTION

Think about this question:

> When do you leave for school?

How many possible answers are there that don't deal with time? That's clearly what the question asker is going for, but students can easily come up with other answers. For instance, given the phrasing, the answer, "After breakfast," would not be an unreasonable answer to expect. Nor would, "When my parents tell me to," be wrong as far as the person *answering* the questionnaire is concerned; these answers just aren't all that useful for the person *asking* the question.

If time is the focus, then make sure the word "time" is in the question. The question,

> What time do you leave home to go to school?

is a better question because it has a *better* focus and is *more specific*.

SOCIAL DESIRABILITY ISSUES

It is really hard to get accurate answers in a survey on topics that people think you have expectations around. Or around things they'd *like* to be better at (because people are telling them it's good to be that way).

A good example from this chapter is the question dealing with recycling. It's a good example of the type of question that people would give a more positive answer for than is actually true—they exaggerate how good they were. Why? Because they either (1) want to look better to you, (2) want to look better to themselves than they are, or (3) both (1) and (2). Sometimes there are ways to address this in how you phrase the question or where you ask it. For example, if there are questions you think people might misrepresent themselves on, having them at the end gets more accurate responses. Other times there are no solutions. In the instance of recycling, you might get a better idea about how much soda or water they drink from plastic bottles if you asked them to keep a log each week (rather than report historical rememberings), but it can be harder to get good individual data on this type of question. In this case, if the people answering the survey are more certain that the results are confidential and cannot be linked back to them, then they might be more honest in their responses.

UNCLEAR INSTRUCTIONS: NUMBER AND TYPE OF RESPONSES

People answering surveys are more likely to give you the responses you want if you indicate clearly in your instructions what you want.

The question,

> How many plastic bottles of water or soda did you drink in the last seven days? (please √)
>
> _____ none _____ (1–5) _____ (6–10) _____ (11–15) _____ (more than 15)

would be *more clear* if you stated,

> Place one checkmark (√) to the left of how many plastic bottles of water or soda you drank in the last seven days.
>
> _____ none _____ (1–5) _____ (6–10) _____ (11–15) _____ (more than 15)

You might not want to provide the instruction in every question if all the questions in a section are similar. In that case you can provide the instructions for the section. That is, in the survey you might have instructions, then the Likert scale listed vertically (as in our example on p. 68), and then a series of statements with a blank after to insert the relevant value from the Likert scale.

> *Question Design Rule #7:* It is *very* wise to test each possible answer to closed-ended questions and ask yourself what the response means *in relation to the question.* Poor questions appear in surveys all the time because the designer has not taken the time to do that. It is an easy check.

THE LOOK OF THE SURVEY OR QUESTIONNAIRE

Questionnaires that are cramped—where as much information is crammed into as little space as is possible—are lacking what is called white space. This is a technical term used by people who design documents, and it is really quite self-explanatory: It refers to parts of a page where nothing is printed. To give you an extreme example, imagine a page with one single-spaced paragraph in a small font. Would you be inclined to read it? What if the same information was put into several shorter paragraphs, in a more readable font? Would you be more inclined to read it then? We bet your answer is "Yes!"

That's the effect white space has. It makes the questionnaire more inviting to read. There are no hard-and-fast rules about this, but after you've printed a trial version of a survey, take a look at it and ask yourself if there is sufficient white space. If not, fiddle with it. If questionnaires are not visually appealing, people are more likely to skip questions, or not answer the survey at all.

THE USE OF DOUBLE-NEGATIVE STATEMENTS

Questions that have double-negatives in them can be very hard to interpret. For instance if you ask someone to indicate if they agree or disagree with the statement,

> I do not dislike oatmeal,

the "disagree" response does *not* mean that the respondent *likes* oatmeal. If your goal is to find out if someone likes oatmeal, then the question that should be asked is

> Do you *agree* or *disagree* (please circle) with the statement "I like oatmeal."

This is a mild example. Using double-negative statements can cause many more difficulties than this and can make it impossible to interpret your data. Quite simply, data that cannot be interpreted effectively may as well not have been collected.

THE USE OF CONTROVERSIAL OR LOADED STATEMENTS

The question,

> Have you stopped kicking your dog when she or he makes you angry? Yes/No

is a loaded question (not to mention a double-barreled one) that is predisposed to the "yes" answer (although how to interpret a "yes" in this case is difficult), although the *main* problem with it is that you assume that the respondent is kicking their dog in the first place. Another example of loading a question would be,

> Do you support lowering speed limits to help save human lives?

which is setting the respondent up to answer "yes" because a "no" answer makes it seem like they don't care about saving human lives. So what's really going on is that this introduces bias into the survey, and no one wants untrustworthy results in a survey.

A better version of the question might be,

> What speed limit do you think highways should have? _____

Or provide some closed-ended responses to choose from indicating different speed limits. Always examine your questions to make sure there are no loaded components.

MISSING CATEGORIES

This is an all too frequent occurrence in closed-ended questions. The person answering the survey can come up with an answer that isn't available in the choices you provided. This puts the respondent in the position of not being able to answer the question *despite having information to contribute*. In this situation, they often leave the question blank. Sometimes they might write it on the side, but since you don't know who else might have chosen this option, the information is reasonably meaningless. Consider the following question:

> How many times have you argued with one or both of your parents since Sunday of this week?
>
> 1. Once.
>
> 2. Two to four times.
>
> 3. Five to ten times.
>
> 4. More than ten times.

Anyone who hasn't argued with their parents at all would have no way to answer the question. Another problem, by the way, is that answers would vary depending on when the respondents were given the survey. To do any comparisons at all you would have to do all of the surveys on the same day, and preferably at the same time.

TOO MANY OR TOO FEW CATEGORIES

This is a judgment call sort of thing, but basically you want to make sure the numbers of categories provides you sufficient, but not too much, information. Consider the question,

Students who are bullying other students should be expelled from the school.

Two categories:

_____ Agree

_____ Disagree

This might not get the range of what students would say if you interviewed them. That's a simple test by the way—as a rule of thumb, if you think that the available categories provide the information you would get if you talked with the respondent about the topic, then you probably have the right number of categories. So how many categories might be too many?

How about this many?

1 = Very, very strongly agree

2 = Very strongly agree

3 = Strongly Agree

4 = Agree

5 = Slightly agree

6 = Neutral

7 = Slightly disagree

8 = Disagree

9 = Strongly disagree

10 = Very strongly disagree

11 = Very, very strongly disagree

Eleven categories is probably overkill. You are making degrees of distinction that provide you little or no more information than a five-point scale would on this topic.

A final note: There are many, many other issues that come up when designing survey questions. We have only listed a few of the main problems here. We encourage you to read more about designing questionnaires online once you and your students have gained some practice at paying attention to the issues discussed here.

CHAPTER 10
SOMEWHAT MORE ADVANCED ANALYSIS OF SURVEY DATA

Most science teachers learned to analyze one type of data in their science programs, *parametric* data (basically, analysis of measures). This is the type of data that you learned to do averages, standard deviations, *t*-tests, ANOVA tests, and so forth with. However, questionnaires provide frequency data, and these are not analyzed using the same approaches because they are *nonparametric* data, and you cannot do those sorts of tests[1] on that sort of data.

This chapter will specifically discuss how to analyze frequency data going beyond using bar graphs and tables to show frequencies. We will mostly discuss Likert scale items (the kind we learned about in the last chapter) in which people are indicating how much they agree or disagree, like or dislike, some statement that was made. First we'll demonstrate how to structure a data table for one of those types of questions (Table 10.1).

You would, of course, make your table with columns 2 to 6 repeated for *each* Likert item in your large data table.

THE PROBLEM OF CENTRAL TENDENCY, OR WHAT WE USUALLY CALL AN AVERAGE

We cannot actually take an arithmetic average for the frequency data we collected with the example Likert item because these kinds of data are distinct from interval-ratio data. This

TABLE 10.1

Example data table for a Likert question "I think cats are the best pets"

(Respondents)	Strongly disagree (1)	Disagree (2)	Neutral (3)	Agree (4)	Strongly agree (5)
			I think cats are the best pets		
0001					√
0002				√	
0003				√	
0004	√				
...					
0020	√				
Total	7	2	3	4	4

1. There are nonparametric equivalents for most of the parametric tests, such as such as the chi-squared test, Mann–Whitney *U* test, Wilcoxon signed-rank test, or Kruskal–Wallis test. (We provide these terms as a starting point for doing more detailed searches on the internet if you actually want to do statistical testing on this type of survey data.)

means that you have to analyze them a little differently. Here's why: You don't really know what the numbers you've assigned to the responses mean. Often people assign numbers 1, 2, 3, 4, 5 to the scale responses and then sum and average those. But you cannot do that. Seriously. It is not defensible mathematically.

The reason is that the assigning of numbers to the scale responses is entirely arbitrary. The categories from "strongly disagree" to "strongly agree" are often numbered 1, 2, 3, 4, and 5 (respectively). The problem is that you could also have assigned the numbers 1, 3, 4, 6, 9—that's also rank order. You have no idea whether the gap is 1 or *less* (because the two possible responses are really close together in the mind of the respondent) for responses that are beside each other than you know whether the gap is 3 or *more*. That means that your normal way of determining the *measure of central tendency* (which we tend to think of as an average) of adding and dividing doesn't really work.

So what do you do? Well, the average for frequency data is what is called a *median* (or, the number in the middle of them all when they're put into order). You *can* report both the arithmetic average and the median—you can even talk about both; and you can even talk about the differences *between* both (if they're not close to each other it suggests the bell curve is "warped" to the right or left [this is called skewness or kurtosis]), which means that the arithmetic stuff *really* doesn't work), but the value with real meaning in this type of data is the median. Let's look at the current example question, "Cats are the best pets," with 20 respondents.

To find the median, let's put all the responses in order:

1, 1, 1, 1, 1, 1, 1, 2, 2, 3, 3, 3, 4, 4, 4, 4, 5, 5, 5, 5

So there were seven "strongly disagree," two "disagree," three "neutral," four "agree," and four "strongly agree" responses. Therefore, the median is the middle value. In the instance (such as this one) in which there are 20 total responses, then the middle number is that at the tenth or eleventh position, so in this case a 3 or, in other words, the "neutral" response on the statement was the median.

In this particular case, that doesn't really seem to tell us much. Let's look at the graph (Figure 10.1).

FIGURE 10.1

Survey response frequencies for the statement "I think cats are the best pets"

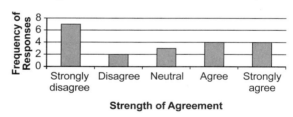

Well, clearly there is stronger disagreement with the statement than agreement since there are more "strongly disagree" responses.

Maybe it would help if we looked at another variable. What if we examined the sex of the student in relation to that question. This is where survey analysis can become quite powerful, when you break down responses in one question in relation to another question.

Teaching Hint: When speaking about frequency data analysis, you might notice that we're not mentioning graphing raw data. That's because you can't. Each bar in the graph represents a count of responses. You can only graph raw data for data that *scatters* around the bar, and the frequency counts do not do that. This means you couldn't use hedging language about a single bar—but you could use hedging language about a pattern *across* the bars.

THE PROBLEM OF COVARYING RELATIONSHIPS WITH FREQUENCY DATA

When dealing with interval-ratio data, figuring out the relationship between variable 1 and variable 2 is not a big deal. You draw a scatterplot and construct a linear model (or line of best fit), which in its simplest version is the equivalent of $y = mx + b$. For that model you even know how to get an idea of how close the model is to describing the data. But how do you understand relationships between variables with frequency data in a survey? That's where crosstabulation tables (or contingency tables) become useful. They are the frequency data equivalent of a scatterplot. Let's look at an example.

In the survey looking at cat data, the sex of respondents was also collected and placed into the larger table. Table 10.2 shows how it would look in that table:

TABLE 10.2

The sexes of respondents to the question "I think cats are the best pets"

(Respondents)	Sex	
	Male	Female
0001		√
0002		√
0003		√
0004	√	
...		
0020	√	
Total	10	10

So, how do we look at the relationship between the variable "sex" as a way of seeing how it related to the frequencies in the "I think cats are the best pets" part of the table? We set up a crosstabulation table. Basically, we'll design a blank table (in this case a 2 × 5 table [described as a two by five table]), and we'll look at the larger data table for the information we need. First, let's combine the two tables (see Table 10.3, p. 80). Then, let's go across each respondent row and determine what sex the respondent was and what level their agreement was with the cat statement. For instance, Respondent 0001 is a "female indicating strongly agree."

TABLE 10.3

A crosstabulation table of the data from the "I think cats are the best pets" survey

(Respondents)	Sex M	Sex F	Strongly disagree	Disagree	Neutral	Agree	Strongly agree
0001 (A)		√					√
0002 (B)		√				√	
0003 (C)		√				√	
0004 (D)	√		√				
...							
0020 (E)	√		√				
Total	10	10	7	2	3	4	4

So what do we do with this information? The crosstabulation table, which is a 2 × 5 table, has two rows (corresponding with male and female) and five columns (corresponding with the five levels of agreeing with the statement). *One* of those cells in that 2 × 5 table (there are 10 cells) corresponds with *both* pieces of information for Respondent 0001 ("female" and "strongly agree"). If you look at Table 10.4(a) on the next page, we've grayed out the cell that corresponds to both of those pieces of information. To complete a crosstabulation table, what you do is put a tic (|) in a cell (see Table 10.4[b]) for *each* time a respondent corresponds

with *that* cell. So in this case, there would be 20 tics distributed in the cells of the table—some cells will end up having many tics, others will have none.

So, what we've done next is (Table 10.4[c]) entered the data on opinions about cats as pets as related to sex using tics by going through the raw data table row by row (from one respondent to the next). Then, we summed the tics in each cell (see Table 10.4[d]) *and* checked the row and column totals against the raw data table. (They should match the number of responses for each variable, in this case sex and cats as pets.)

TABLE 10.4

A crosstabulation table for sex and "I think cats are the best pets"

(a) The cell corresponding with "female who strongly agrees" is grayed out.

	Strongly disagree	Disagree	Neutral	Agree	Strongly agree
Male					
Female					

(b) The cell corresponding with "female who strongly agrees" has the tic entered in it; this represents Respondent 0001.

	Strongly disagree	Disagree	Neutral	Agree	Strongly agree
Male					
Female						

(c) The cells are filled out for all 20 respondents. Respondents 0001 to 0004 and 0020 have their tics replaced with letters A to E (all the other data are tics).

	Strongly disagree	Disagree	Neutral	Agree	Strongly agree
Male	DE | | | | |	| |	|		
Female			| |	BC| |	A| | |

(d) Tics are replaced with cell totals, and totals are checked against the original table.

	Strongly disagree	Disagree	Neutral	Agree	Strongly agree	Total
Male	7	2	1			10
Female			2	4	4	10
Total	7	2	3	4	4	20

Okay, so all the totals match the raw data table. This tells us that we've entered everything correctly. It's pretty useful to check things this way.

So what do we notice in this table?

First, we can see there's a definite sex pattern. Most male students disagree with the statement that cats make the best pets, whereas most female students agree with the statement. It's a pretty obvious pattern, and given that it's so strong you could refer to it as a significant pattern (unlike before when it was not possible to use hedging language for a single column response, you can use it when discussing patterns, depending on how strong the pattern is).

However, on the basis of our experience teaching people to do this, we can bet that you're still unclear on how a crosstabulation table is the frequency data equivalent of a scatterplot for understanding patterns between variables. So let's look at another example, one for which we're doing a 5 × 5 (five by five) crosstabulation comparing the responses to two five-point Likert items.

We'll look at responses to the two Likert items:

> I think cats are the best pets.

and

> I think dogs are the best pets.

We will *just* show the part of the larger data table that shows the data for those two items (Table 10.5).

TABLE 10.5

A table showing how respondents answered questions about whether cats or dogs are the best pets

(Respondents)	I think cats are the best pets					I think dogs are the best pets				
	Strongly disagree	Disagree	Neutral	Agree	Strongly agree	Strongly disagree	Disagree	Neutral	Agree	Strongly agree
0001					√		√			
0002				√		√				
0003				√				√		
0004	√								√	
...										
0020	√									√
Total	7	2	3	4	4	3	4	5	2	6

We can now construct a 5 × 5 crosstabulation table to examine the data set for any relationship between these two items. The "lowest" response (i.e., "strongly disagree") is put in the lower left of the table (just like the lower numbers are usually in the bottom left of a scatterplot) (Table 10.6).

TABLE 10.6

A table showing how respondents answered questions about whether cats or dogs are the best pets

I think cats are the best pets	Total	3	4	5	2	6	
	Strongly agree	| |	| |				4
	Agree	|	|	|		|	4
	Neutral			| |	|		3
	Disagree					| |	2
	Strongly disagree		|	| |	|	| | |	7
		Strongly disagree	Disagree	Neutral	Agree	Strongly agree	Total

I think dogs are the best pets

So, what do we do with this table?

We can note that there are clusters of tics in the top left and the bottom right. But the clusters are kind of broad. This relationship down and to the right means it's an inverse relationship, which means that, in general, if respondents answered one way for the dog, they answered the opposite way for the cat. This is *not*, however, a very strong relationship. A strong relationship would mostly have

tics across the single row of diagonal boxes, a less strong relationship would mostly have tics across the *wider* diagonal line (which is ~3 boxes wide). The more tics there are away from whatever line is visible, the weaker the relationship is. Let's look at a grayed out version of the line visible for this data (Table 10.7).

TABLE 10.7

The width of the grayed-out portion of the graph shows that there is a weak inverse relationship between those who like cats and those who like dogs

I think cats are the best pets	Total	3	4	5	2	6	
	Strongly agree	| |	| |				4
	Agree	|	|	|		|	4
	Neutral			| |	|		3
	Disagree					| |	2
	Strongly disagree		|	| |	|	| | |	7
		Strongly Disagree	Disagree	Neutral	Agree	Strongly Agree	Total

I think dogs are the best pets

When you look at it with the shaded cells, you can see that 16 of the 20 tics lie along the broad line running from top left to bottom right. This means that there is an inverse relationship, although not a strong one, between thinking that dogs make the best pets and thinking that cats make the best pet. Generally people think one or the other, but not both. In some ways this makes sense because you couldn't think that both made the best pet. If you count the tics in the top-left four boxes and the bottom-right four boxes you might also conclude that support for cats and dogs is reasonably equal. Finally, there is *one* respondent who strongly disagrees that cats are the best pet and disagrees that dogs are the best pet. You could conclude that this person probably thinks that some other animal makes the best pet, although it's somewhat possible (it's difficult to tell with the phrasing) that they just don't think much of pets in general.

As you can see, doing crosstabulations can add a considerable amount to your data analysis. They can be as small as 2 × 2 in size or as big as the data allows (technically, a 1 × 2 table would be a frequency table). There is, by the way, a simple way to enhance these crosstabulation tables even further and provide information for an even more detailed analysis.

In our demonstration of constructing a crosstabulation table, we put tics in each cell for each intersection between items. Rather than using a tic, you could use a symbol that related to a third variable. For instance, if you knew that respondents 0001 and 0002 were males, you could insert an M instead of a tic. If respondents 0003, 0004, and 0020 were females, you could insert an F instead of a tic. If we did that for all respondents, then the crosstabulation table would look like Table 10.8.

This structuring of the table for a third variable, sex, indicates that there is strong sex-based clustering with males generally thinking dogs are the best pets, not cats, whereas females generally think that cats are the best pets, not dogs. Adding this level of complexity

TABLE 10.8

A crosstabulation table using F for female and M for male to show the respondents to the questions about whether cats or dogs are better pets

		Strongly Disagree	Disagree	Neutral	Agree	Strongly Agree	Total
	Total	3	4	5	2	6	
I think cats are the best pets	Strongly agree	FF	FF				4
	Agree	F	F	F		F	4
	Neutral			FM	F		3
	Disagree					MM	2
	Strongly disagree		M	MM	M	MMM	7
		I think dogs are the best pets					

in the analysis is probably best left for more advanced (and, dare we say, older) students.

SCALE CONSTRUCTION

So far you've been mostly working with frequency data in your analysis. Earlier we pointed out that you could not use parametric types of analysis on this type of data. However, there *is* an exception to this, and the exception is that *in some circumstances* you can create interval-ratio-level data from the frequency data obtained from Likert questions (see p. 68), and then you can do higher-order analysis such as averages, *t*-tests, ANOVA tests, regression analysis, and so forth with your survey data.

First, we're going to say that we don't recommend that you have any students other than upper-level students do this. When you work with ordinal-level data (ordered categories) from a statistical analysis perspective there is only minimal ability to compare responses between questions. When examining Likert responses you normally obtain frequencies for the strength of responses. Consider the question in Table 10.9 from a survey given to dog owners:

TABLE 10.9

Survey given to dog owners

I think dogs are the best pets						
Strongly disagree	A	B	C	D	E	Strongly agree

This is just one single question about dogs. What if there was another question?

> I've had a dog I've thought of as my best friend.

And another question,

> My best memories as a child were about me and my dog.

Each of these questions could be summarized in a frequency bar chart (such as is discussed in Chapter 3).

But there's a bigger picture here about dogs that can be addressed. If someone answered "strongly agree" to all three questions and you noticed that, what would you conclude that meant? If I knew someone who thought "dogs are the best pets," whose "dog is [his or her] best friend," and whose "best memories are about [his or her] dog," I'd think they were someone who *really* liked dogs. A lot. A whole lot. More than most people. A dog fanatic, almost.

How might we use this information in a research project?

Right now we just have three questions about dogs, and each tells us something about each specific person, and overall we could look at the frequencies for each question for each type of response. For starters, let's look at a table that accomplishes that for 10 people who were surveyed (Table 10.10).

TABLE 10.10

A table showing frequencies for each question for each type of response

Subject	Importance of dogs		
	Q1	Q2	Q3
1	E	E	E
2	B	C	C
3	C	B	C
4	C	C	B
5	A	A	B
6	E	D	D
7	A	B	A
8	D	C	E
9	C	D	B
10	A	C	E
Number of responses	SD = 3 1 3 1 SA = 2	SD = 1 2 4 2 SA = 1	SD = 1 3 2 1 SA = 3

You'll note that we've put the dog fanatic as the first subject. This table represents the responses of 10 people to those three questions (of course, surveys will have other questions; we'll get to that). You can see that from a summary perspective we could create the three graphs shown in Figure 10.2.

Those graphs show us the responses to each individual question about dogs. But there is a bigger picture that can be looked at here by combining these questions into a scale that looks at the importance of dogs (there's also another set of data for questions where "dogs" was replaced with "cats" in questions 1–3; you could make an Importance of Cats scale from those questions).

Remember the dog fanatic who responded "strongly agree" to all three questions? What happens if we change the table responses to numeric (A = 1, B = 2, C = 3, D = 4, E = 5) and then summed them along the row? The total would be 15 for the dog fanatic (Table 10.11)

In survey research, this summing across columns is called *scale construction*.[2] Sometimes researchers do parametric analysis on ordinal data (because some required conditions are met), but most often it is inappropriate to do this and should not be done (as we have mentioned several times earlier). *However*, once you have a number of related survey questions all addressing some central concept (such as importance of dogs or importance of cats), then there's a way to construct parametric data from nonparametric data (i.e., frequencies) so that higher-order analysis can be done—such as averaging, standard deviations, *t*-tests, and ANOVA tests (Table 10.11).

By summing the item scores across all three dog questions you can calculate an overall Importance of Dogs score, which can be considered the equivalent of an interval-ratio variable

2. We are using what is called "face validity" to choose the questions to sum together here. Basically, we're looking at them and saying, "Yup, they seem to be addressing the same sort of thing." In real scale construction, you would do a Cronbach's alpha calculation to see if the questions hang together response-wise, followed by a confirmatory factor analysis. This level of analysis is not necessary for surveys designed and used by kids.

FIGURE 10.2

Graphs showing responses to questions about the importance of dogs

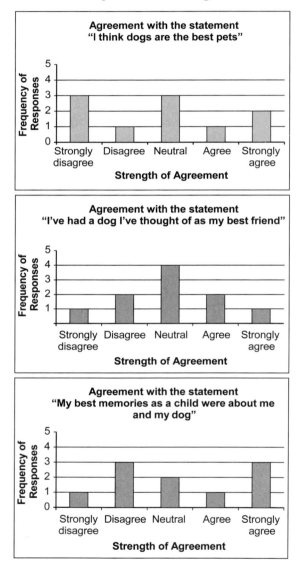

TABLE 10.11

A table used to construct parametric data from nonparametric data

Subject	Importance of dogs				Importance of cats			
	Q1	Q2	Q3	Sum	Q1	Q2	Q3	Sum
1	5	5	5	15	1	1	1	3
2	2	3	3	8	3	2	2	7
3	3	2	3	8	1	2	2	5
4	3	3	2	8	1	1	2	4
5	1	1	2	4	5	5	4	14
6	5	4	4	13	3	3	3	13
7	1	2	1	4	4	5	5	14
8	4	3	5	12	1	3	2	6
9	3	4	2	9	2	2	1	5
10	1	3	5	9	2	2	2	6
and so on...								

score. The greater data range (3–15 in the above example) allows a closer approximation to a normal standard curve and therefore allows the data to be treated as interval-ratio data.

For instance, you could now do a *t*-test to see if there were statistical differences between the Importance of Dogs compared to the Importance of Cats scales. Or you could plot a scatterplot and do a correlation analysis with *r*-squared to see if there is a relationship between how people think about cats and how they think about dogs.

DIRECTIONALITY OF QUESTIONS (THE BIG MISTAKE IN CREATING A SUMMED SCALE)

There is *one* big mistake that people make in creating a scale that we think you need to be cautioned about. You have to bear this in mind: The questions all have to be the same *"direction."*

You *cannot* construct a scale using questions where the *higher score is opposite* of what your big scale idea is about *unless* you correct the scale by reversing it, and sometimes that is difficult to do.

Consider the following questions:

Q1: I think dogs are the best pets.

Q2: I've had a dog I've thought of as my best friend.

Q3: My best memories as a child
were *not* about me and my dog.

If you had responses from this scale,

1 = Strongly disagree

2 = Disagree

3 = Neutral

4 = Agree

5 = Strongly agree

then a "strongly agree" response to Q1 and Q2 would be consistent with having a positive attitude about dogs in general. But a "strongly agree" to Q3 would *not* indicate a positive attitude about dogs in general. If you just added all three responses together (5 + 5 + 5) you'd get a *very* strong "dog attitude" sum of 15, *but* it would be misrepresentative because the response to Q3 was not positive about memories of dogs.

How is this dealt with? By reversing the question scores. In this case, the response to Q3 is reversed to a score of 1 (if it was an "agree" response it would be reversed to a value of 2). This means that the sum of the three questions is now 5 + 5 + 1 = 11, which is a high "dog attitude" summed score, but not the highest possible (which is what you had before the question reversal).

If you are going to reverse the score of a question, you should make sure (by careful reading) that the reversed question actually warrants that score. In this case, we're reasonably comfortable with Q3 being reversed, but for some questions this can be an issue. This ends up being a judgment call (there are no hard-and-fast rules when designing a survey this way), so make sure that if you're phrasing a question you think will need reversing that you have checked to make sure that the reversal makes logical sense.

AFTERWORD

We know you probably haven't read this book from front to back, but we didn't expect you to, so don't worry. We tried to make each section more or less stand-alone so that you didn't have to do that.

However, if you have eventually made it through the entire book, you'll have a background (with this book as a resource) that will enable you to make better sense of reports and data you run across in your job, and you'll also be able to help most students with most types of projects they'll encounter in their schooling, all the way from early grades up to senior students working on science fair projects.

Making sense of data properly and effectively is a key skill in science literacy. We're glad you took some steps to help you and your students achieve that. Also, make sure you check back at the NSTA Press website (*www.nsta.org/publications/press*) every now and then. We're going to work with them to provide more resources for you to use with your classes, including creating web pages that will allow your students to do simple statistical analyses if they're doing inquiry investigations.

Also, we strongly encourage you to look over the appendixes. There are lots of useful resources in there, including photocopy masters of assignments or worksheets you could use with your students.

Finally, both of us frequently attend the national NSTA conference, and we're happy to talk with you about any issues you came across when using the book. We'll incorporate those into future editions. We're also happy to add new sections in the future if you have any suggestions about those.

All the best,

Michael Bowen
Mount Saint Vincent University
Halifax, Nova Scotia

A. W. Bartley
Lakehead University
Thunder Bay, Ontario

APPENDIX I
CLASS WORKSHEETS FOR MARBLE-ROLLING ACTIVITIES

MARBLE-ROLLING LAB ACTIVITY SETUP

In these activities, students roll a marble through a hole cut into various types of cups and graph how far the cups are pushed (Figure A1.1).

BASIC EQUIPMENT SETUP

Note the following:

1. The basic setup of the equipment is the same for each activity.

2. The ruler has a groove down the middle, and it is best if it doesn't have any binder holes (*Note:* Business supply stores often carry these types of rulers).

3. It is helpful if the data collection sheet is held to the table by masking tape.

4. A small piece of clay can be used to hold the ruler in place.

5. We often give students a height range for the book stack, thus stacking the environment (see Teaching Hint on p. 24) so that students are arguing for their own answers rather than being worried if their distances are identical to others.

FIGURE A1.1

General setup of the "measurement tool" for the marble rolling lab

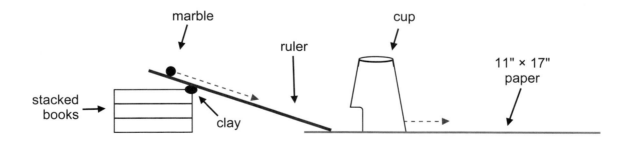

DATA SHEET LAYOUT

Note the following:

1. The baseline should be far enough from the front edge of the page so that no cups overhang the edge.

2. The tics should be far enough from the edges of the page so that the cups do not slide off the paper itself while they are moving.

3. If you are taping two pieces of 8½" × 11" paper together to get that 11" × 17" size, then you should make sure the seam overlaps so that the cup doesn't catch on the edge of the second sheet of paper.

Activity #1: Cup Type Activity (Figure A1.2)
Visit *www.youtube.com/watch?v=4INACB11rxU* to see the setup for Activity #1.

FIGURE A1.2

Data sheet for the cup type activity

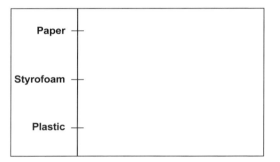

Activity #2: Cup Size Activity (Figure A1.3)
Visit *www.youtube.com/watch?v=T2OWzYQaH S4* for a video of Activity #2.

FIGURE A1.3

Data sheet for the cup size activity

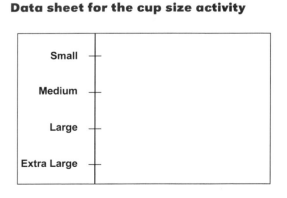

Activity #3: Stacked Cup Activity (Figure A1.4)

FIGURE A1.4

Data sheet for the stacked cup activity

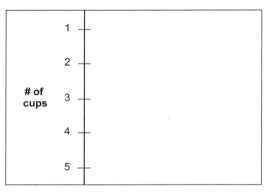

MARBLE-ROLLING LAB ACTIVITY 1

FOCUS QUESTION

How does the type of cup affect how far a cup is pushed by the marble? (*Note:* **Type does not mean the size but the material the cup is made from.)**

1. Set up your equipment as has been demonstrated at the front of the room. Remember to put a baseline on the recording paper so that the leading edges of the cups all start at the same place. Choose three cups of different materials, cut a hole in the side (see the example cups at the front) if you need to.

2. Determine your list of *controlled variables* (the things you try and keep the same so it's a fair test of all of the cups).

3. Conduct a number of trials sufficiently big so that you can effectively argue you have demonstrated and accounted for the *range of possible variations in outcome.*

   Using the data on your recording paper, consider the following:

   - How could you illustrate the average distance traveled by each type of cup?

   - What type of graph could you use to easily show the differences between cups?

   - How might you illustrate the range for each cup that you would be comfortable saying most marble rolls would push the cup to?

4. Answer the following questions:

   i. What physics-like word might describe what's happening between the cup and the desk surface that might be affecting the outcome? (It's the same word that would explain why you can go so fast when you ice-skate on a frozen pond but not when you try to snowboard down a grassy hill.)

   ii. What features of the cups might be affecting that factor? Make a list of as many as you can think of. Look carefully at the parts of the cup touching the data paper.

   iii. What one thing might you change so that the cups slide differently (farther or less far)?

   iv. How might you improve your ability to express the arguments for average and range so that you could tell your cousin Jenny about what you did over the phone?

MARBLE-ROLLING LAB ACTIVITY 2

FOCUS QUESTION
How does the size of the cup affect how far a cup is pushed by the marble?

Note: What do you think is the most important feature of the cups to keep the same? What other controlled variables are important so that a fair test is possible? What variables can you control in this study that it was not possible to control in the last study? What variables might you not be able to control that could make interpreting the data somewhat difficult?

1. Set up your equipment as demonstrated at the front of the room (remember to draw the baseline and the tics). Don't forget to put the cups in order of size on the paper from smallest to largest (left to right).

2. Conduct a number of trials so that you can effectively argue you have sufficiently demonstrated and accounted for the range of possible variations in outcome. Check with other groups around you as to whether they are convinced by your data and to see if they think you've done enough trials.

3. Using the data on your data sheet, answer the following questions:

   - How could you illustrate the average distance traveled by each size of cup?

   - How might you best illustrate the pattern that you can see from smallest to largest?

   - Can you predict what the values would be for cup sizes between the sizes you used using a graph like this? Why or why not?

   - What physical feature could you measure about the different cups that would allow you to change your *x*-axis so you could do those sorts of predictions?

   - What conclusions can you draw from the data you collected?

   - Cups of different sizes have different masses. How could you change cup mass without really changing other features so that you could look at consistent patterns of cup mass and the distance the cup moved?

   - Try and think of a real-world example of what you've just studied in this activity. How might this information be useful to you?

MARBLE-ROLLING LAB ACTIVITY 3

FOCUS QUESTIONS

A. What is the relationship between the number of cups in the stack and how far the stack is pushed? (*Note:* **You get to pick the cup size and type.**)

B. Is the relationship linear or nonlinear?

1. Set up your equipment in the way your class decided would make your measurement tool more standardized. (The class should decide these rules and write them on the board.)

2. Don't forget to record the data on the graph paper *in order* from one cup to four cups (in the stack, left to right) along the baseline you've drawn. Put six equally spaced tics across that line (starting with a zero tic on the far left [see the example at front of the classroom]).

3. Conduct the minimum number of trials agreed upon in your class discussion so that you can *effectively* argue you have sufficiently demonstrated and accounted for a clear pattern in the outcome. Check with other groups around you as to whether they are convinced by your data.

4. Using the data on your graph paper, answer the following questions:

    - How might you best illustrate the pattern that you can see from smallest to largest stack? I bet you're thinking about a line of some sort. Would the best trend line be one that was curved or straight?

    - Can you predict how far two and a half cups would be pushed? How would you do this?

    - After you have figured out how to predict how far two and a half cups would be pushed, think about how *sure* you are about your prediction. Are you comfortable with stating a single value? Would you bet your MP3 player or cell phone that you were exactly right?

    - Draw a trend bar (as demonstrated at the front) and think about it instead of your trend line. How would you use it to predict how far two and a half cups would be pushed? How certain would you be that the result would be on the trend line? How certain would you be that the range would be in the range of the trend bar?

    - Predict how far five cups would go. Test your prediction.

The number of cups is an example of what a scientist would call a *mass unit*. How could you make your mass units in this study a more accurate measure? Would improving the accuracy of your mass units improve the precision of your trend line? Why or why not? Is improving the *precision* of your trend line the same as making your trend bar narrower? What effect would this have on your prediction of two and a half cups?

5. Consider the above issues by examining the variability in the holes cut into the lip of the cups you have used.

MARBLE-ROLLING LAB ACTIVITY 4

1. Determine a focus question. What variable are you going to look at? If you're stuck, take a look at number 7 in Marble Rolling Lab Activity 1 for ideas.

2. As a class, determine what you are going to standardize with the study so that different groups can compare findings if they study similar factors. *Note*: Although one would normally complete a vee-map *while* you did your study, in this case you are expected to do them individually for homework.

3. Set up your equipment in the way your class decided to make your measurement tool more standardized.

4. Conduct the minimum number of trials agreed upon in your class discussion so that you can *effectively* argue you have sufficiently demonstrated and accounted for a clear pattern in the outcome. Check with other groups around you as to whether they are convinced by your data.

5. Complete the vee map for homework to submit next day.

APPENDIX II
OTHER SCAFFOLDED INVESTIGATION ACTIVITIES

In Chapters 3–5 we described a series of marble rolling activities that can be used to teach students the fundamentals of the three different data types (nominal, ordinal, and interval-ratio). We think that working students through each of these activities will help develop their understanding of the relationship between the different data types and the basic kinds of graphs that can be used with them.

You should note that the basic structure of the marble rolling activity can be modified to address other data literacy issues and science concepts, so you could modify this activity to teach about the different data types and the associated graphs. For instance, students could

- modify the surface the cups are sliding across (plastic, paper, cardboard);
- raise or lower the height of the ramp (one, two, or three books, and so on);
- use different sizes or masses of marbles; and
- change the mass of the cups by adding modeling clay.

There are other potential modifications too. However, many other sorts of activities could be used to accomplish the same goal (and might be more appropriate for the age of students or the specific curriculum you teach). Below, we list a few lessons that can be used to help scaffold your students to similar insights about the order of variables and the different types of graphs associated with them. There are two different types of activities; in some the actual data are drawn right onto the paper that the graph can then be drawn on (as with the marble rolling activities), in others the task

is more experience distant, and the students have to collect the data using an instrument (a meter ruler, a stopwatch, and so on) or conduct counts, so the activities are somewhat more abstract.

ACTIVITIES IN WHICH THE DATA ARE DIRECTLY MARKED ONTO PAPER (I.E., EXPERIENCE NEAR)

- Buoyancy of pencils (the effect of solutes)
- The ball bounce activity
- The elastic stretch activity
- Temperature effects on balloon size

ACTIVITIES IN WHICH THE DATA ARE ENTERED IN TABLES (I.E., MORE EXPERIENCE DISTANT)

- Factors affecting the germination success of seeds
- Paper helicopter drop activity
- Soil moisture and distance from trees
- How fast does it dissolve?

We have provided reasonable detail of how to conduct these activities, but we suggest that the analysis follow the principles and approaches discussed with the marble rolling activities in Chapters 3–5.

BUOYANCY OF PENCILS: THE EFFECT OF SOLUTES

Description: This activity has students exploring factors around flotation of an object depending on differences in the solute and/or solvent. The amount of flotation is determined by the relative densities of the solution versus the floating object. The ordinal study may address a student misconception (the floating height should be constant).

	Nominal	Ordinal	Interval-ratio
Overview	Comparing how high a pencil floats in two test tubes, each with a *different solution* (we suggest using equal amounts of sugar in one and salt in the other).	Comparing how high a pencil floats in test tubes with *different amounts of solvent* (we suggest water) in them.	Comparing how high a pencil floats in test tubes with *different amounts of a dissolved solute* (we suggest sugar dissolved in water).
Detail	Students put two test tubes side by side in a test tube holder. They put an equal amount of water in each and add equal amounts of sugar to one and salt to the other. They then float their shortened pencil (with a tack on the end and a thread allowing them to remove the pencil) and mark on the Bristol board where the tack floats up to. The baseline for comparison is drawn where the liquid surface is found before the pencil is put in it.	Students fill five test tubes in a rack with increasing amounts of water (from about one-third full to almost full). A baseline is drawn on the Bristol board at the *lowest* level. The Bristol board *must* be raised for each test tube when the height of the pencil is being measured so that the baseline is at the level of the water before the pencil is put in it. A mark is placed on the Bristol board for each test tube at the height at which the tack in the pencil floats.	The first test tube has water only. The second through fifth test tubes have equal multiples of a solute (e.g., sugar amounts) put into them (so, 0x, 1x, 2x, 3x, 4x the base amount of solute). The baseline is at the water level before the pencil is put in. For each test tube, a tic is placed on the baseline and the amount of solute recorded there. The height the tack floats to in each test tube is then marked on the Bristol board.

FIGURE A2.1

Buoyancy of pencils activity setup

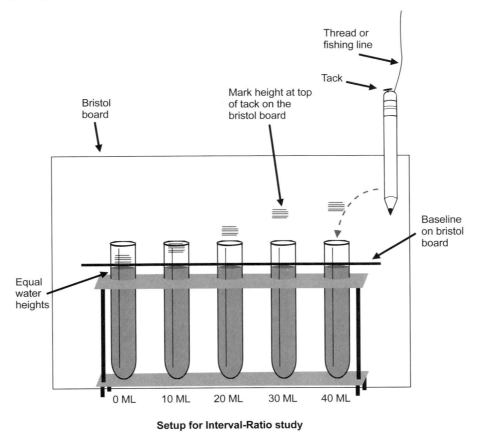

Setup for Interval-Ratio study

ADDITIONAL NOTES

1. Supplies: Bristol board (cut to smaller pieces, see diagram for rough size), test tubes, test tube racks, wooden pencils (preferably with eraser on end), thread, sugar, salt, and water.

2. The measures of the sugar, salt, and so on can be in milliliters, grams, teaspoons, number of packets or cubes, and so forth, just so long as they are the same (as in the nominal study) or change appropriately (as in the interval-ratio study).

3. The baseline on the paper stays even with the equal level of the water solution for the nominal and interval-ratio study. The paper must be moved in the ordinal study so that the baseline is always at the level of the water and the pencil height is recorded in relation to that starting point.

4. Prior to class, the teacher will have to play with amounts of salt or sugar needed, which varies depending on test tube size (and pencil length).

THE BALL-BOUNCE ACTIVITY

Description: This activity had students dropping different balls onto the floor and examining how high they bounce. We use a sheet of Bristol board as a backboard and to mark the bounce height.

	Nominal	Ordinal	Interval-ratio
Overview	Comparing how high *different types* of balls bounce (e.g., Ping Pong ball, golf ball, and tennis ball).	Comparing the bounce of small, medium, and large balls made of the *same type of material* (e.g., rubber).	Comparing how high a single ball bounces when being *dropped from different heights*.
Details	Mark a drop line near to one edge of the Bristol board. Tape the Bristol board to a wall with the "drop line" horizontal and at the highest level. The bottom of the Bristol board should touch the floor. Drop each ball several times. The number of times you do this depends on the results; repeat until you are comfortable with consistency within the results (see Data Literacy Comment 3.2, p. 20 for more). For the next ball, move the starting point a few centimeters to the right on the drop line. Repeat the experiment. Ball 3 should be a few more centimeters to the right (all three balls should be equally spaced from each other on the baseline).	This is a similar setup to the nominal experiment except that you are using balls made out of the same material. The procedure is the same, except the order on the baseline is related to the increasing size of the balls.	This part requires measurement using a meter ruler and a single ball. Tape the Bristol board to the wall. Mark a point to the left of center base of the Bristol board. Measure 20 cm across and 20 cm up; mark this with an "x"; it is your drop point. Drop the ball from there, and mark the height it bounces to with an "x" in a different color. Do this several times until you get consistent results. For the second drop point, move 30 cm across and 30 cm up. Collect the data in the same manner as for 20 cm. Continue the increase of 10 cm across and 10 cm up. Repeat until you have at least five drop heights.

FIGURE A2.2

Ball-bounce activity setup

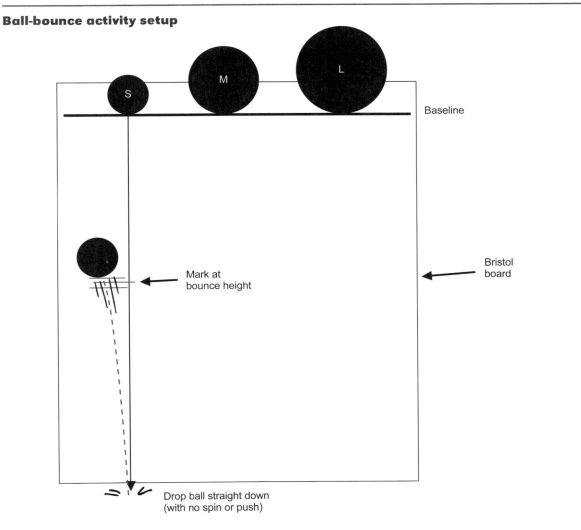

ADDITIONAL NOTES

1. Supplies: A collection of different balls, some sheets of Bristol board, a pencil, and a yard stick or meter ruler.

2. The number of times students drop the balls to collect their results depends upon their ability to make a clean drop with no spin or push. (See Data Literacy Comment 3.2, p. 20.)

3. In the nominal and the ordinal study, the bounce height should be marked at the bottom of the ball because the balls are aligned along the bottom on the baseline before they are dropped.

ELASTIC-STRETCH ACTIVITY

Description: This activity has the students examining the effect of mass on the extension of elastics. The activity requires several different elastic bands, a collection of pennies for use as weights, a Styrofoam cup for use as a basket, two loops of string, and two paper clips to attach the cup to the elastic. The elastic should be supported by a string tied to a meter ruler between two desks and the data collected by marking the amount the elastic is stretched onto Bristol board.

	Nominal	Ordinal	Interval-ratio
Overview	Comparing two elastic bands of the *same diameter but with different widths* (e.g., one thick elastic and one thin elastic) to see how far they stretch with the same amount of weight.	Two options: Comparing three elastics (or more) that are close to the same thickness but are different diameters. Compare three elastics that are close to the *same diameter, but different thicknesses*.	Comparing how far a single elastic *stretches with different amount of weight*.
Details	Set up the equipment as in the diagram. Attach the thick elastic to the support string and then add the cup. Mark the top of the cup on the Bristol board and draw a baseline across that point. Put 25 pennies into the cup, and watch it extend and settle. Mark the top of the cup in its new position on the Bristol board. Remove the coins and allow the elastic to settle, mark the point again. Repeat the experiment with the thin elastic.	Set up the experiment as shown in the diagram, and complete as in the nominal activity for each diameter of elastic. *Note*: The baseline should be moved to be at the top of the cup for each elastic so that only the amount of "stretch" is being compared.	Make marks at 0, 10, 20, 30, 40, and 50 cm along a line near the top of the Bristol board. Set up the system as in the diagram. Place the top of the empty hanging cup at the 0 cm point and mark an "x" on the Bristol board. Move the setup to the 10 cm point, add 10 coins, and let the cup settle. Mark the position of the top of the cup on the Bristol board. Move the cup along for each trial, and mark the position of the top of the cup for 20, 30, 40, and finally, 50 coins.

FIGURE A2.3

Elastic-stretch activity setup

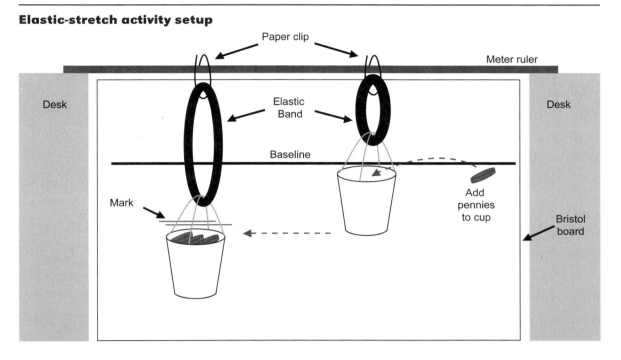

ADDITIONAL NOTES

1. You will need to look carefully at the elastics and how they extend when the pennies are added. You don't want the elastics so thick that there are not sufficient changes for small numbers of coins, nor so thin that the extension is too great and the cup touches the floor or table when 50 coins are added.

2. *Safety goggles* are necessary here.

3. Office supply stores usually offer a good range of rubber bands. For example, Staples 3 ½" rubber bands (#19 [3 ½" × ¹⁄₁₆"]; #33 [3 ½" × ⅛"]; and #64 [3 ½" × ¼"]) provide a good range of elastics for this activity.

TEMPERATURE, LIGHT, AND RADIATION EFFECTS ON BALLOON SIZE

Description: This activity has students exploring the factors that can cause balloons to contract and expand, which relates to the kinetic theory of matter (or what some textbooks call the kinetic-molecular theory of matter) and electromagnetic radiation (light, specifically absorption and reflection).

	Nominal	Ordinal	Interval-ratio
Overview	Comparing the expansion (or contraction) of a white with a black balloon. Two studies are possible: one study is done by placing the balloons in the sun, the other by placing them in the freezer. (The one in the sun is easier to interpret for younger children; the one in the freezer might be used to challenge older students.)	Comparing the final size of balloons that started at the same size and shape placed in different temperatures (ranked but unknown from a measured perspective).	Comparing the final size of balloons that started at the same size and shape placed in different temperatures (temperature is recorded in each location, the *x*-axis scaled in an interval-ratio fashion, and data recorded according to the temperature).
Details	Have students blow up two balloons, one black and one white, of the same size and shape to the same diameter. Place the same dimension (width?) along "baseline 1," drawn on an 11" × 17" piece of paper. Have them draw a line at the widest part of each balloon and label it as baseline 2. This is where the bars are drawn from.	Have students place four balloons of the same color, size, and shape in a freezer (coldest), a fridge (cold), on a table in the classroom (normal), or in a window in the sun (warmer) after a baseline width has been established (see nominal experiment). Place them into their different temperature regimes for 5 to 10 minutes, remove them one by one, and mark their width again at the appropriate tic. Note that for this ordinal study, the tics on the axis for each location should be the same distance apart.	The basic instructions for data collection are the same as for the ordinal study. *Note*: The *x*-axis is scaled according to the temperature (such that it is evenly spaced between each degree. For instance, 10, 15, 20, 25, and 30°C tics are all the same distance apart). Students record the new balloon width at the place on the *x*-axis corresponding to the temperature where the balloon was being "treated."

FIGURE A2.4

Balloon size activity setup

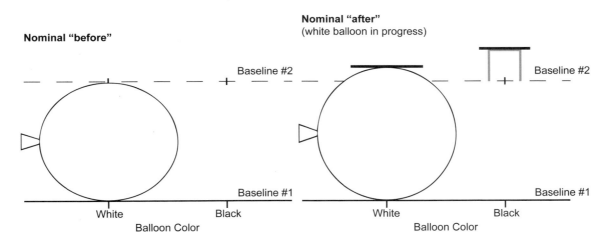

ADDITIONAL NOTES

1. Supplies: 11" × 17" (or two regular sheets of paper taped together) and a thermometer (for the interval-ratio study).

2. The activity could be done by having the teacher recording the temperature data in each location and then providing it to the students.

3. *Note:* This activity does not require data to be recollected for the interval-ratio study. The students *could* use the same data collected in the ordinal study but with the *x*-axis now scaled for the temperature data, thus allowing extrapolation and interpolation.

FACTORS AFFECTING THE GERMINATION SUCCESS OF SEEDS

Description: This activity has students exploring the factors that affect the germination success of seeds. Germination is when you try to grow a seed into a plant by making it damp or wet. Germination success is usually defined as a small sprout or rootlet emerging from the seed case.

	Nominal	Ordinal	Interval-ratio
Overview	Comparing germination success between *two different types of seeds of similar sizes*.	Comparing germination success between *seeds of different sizes from different types of plants*.	Comparing the *effect of presoaking* on germination success of one type of seed (large types may be better).
Details	Sprout (10? 20?) seeds on filter paper in petri dishes (or some other standardized approach). After a predetermined period of time (usually a few days), count the number of seeds with sprouts or rootlets emerging from the seed cases, enter in a table, and graph. The moisture conditions at start and the presoaking time are the controlled variables.	Choose four or five types of seeds of different sizes. When drawing your graph, list the names of the seeds on the *x*-axis in increasing order of their average *size* as they go from left to right. This allows the drawing of a line graph depicting germination success as it might relate to the size of seeds. Depending on the seeds chosen, there may not be a pattern.	Pick one type of seed. Five hours before your germination "start time," set 10 or 20 seeds soaking. Each hour after that, start another batch of seeds soaking. At 0 hour, put each set of seeds (5, 4, 3, 2, 1, and 0 hours presoaking) into your germination equipment. After the predetermined time for your seed type, count the number of successful germinations and graph on a scatterplot.

FIGURE A2.5

Success of seeds activity setup

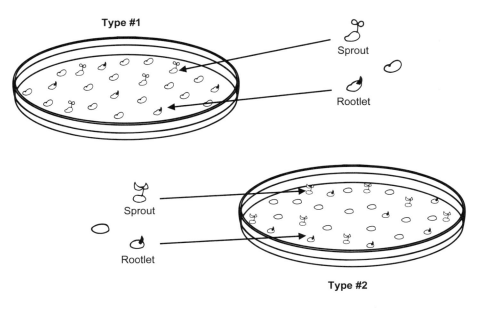

Count sprouts and rootlets and enter in table
to compare the two types of seeds

ADDITIONAL NOTES

1. These activities are slightly more abstract than those in which the students mark the data directly on paper because the students have to count the number of seeds. (See the previous page for details.)

2. The teacher might have to conduct some testing of seeds that they obtain to make sure that they sprout. *Note*: Some seed types require some presoaking.

3. Different seeds need different amounts of moisture to germinate successfully. Teachers might want to look into this in advance.

4. Determining average seed size could have students measuring the length or weight of seeds to determine an average.

5. Seeds are often available from bulk food stores. Chick peas (also known as garbanzo beans), wheat seeds, mung bean seeds, radish seeds, mustard seeds, and alfalfa seeds all work well for these activities.

PAPER HELICOPTER DROP ACTIVITY

Description: This activity has students exploring factors related to dropping a paper helicopter and timing how long it takes to hit the floor. We've tried to pick variables that relate to science ideas that students think about so that those enter into their explanation of patterns. For instance, they might think that black paper might be warmer and therefore fall more slowly because of rising air currents (caused by the heating) around it.

	Nominal	Ordinal	Interval-ratio
Overview	Comparing times for dropping two helicopters that are made from papers *of two different colors* (e.g., black and white).	Comparing times for dropping paper helicopters made from *different weights or thicknesses of paper*.	Comparing times for dropping paper helicopters with *different numbers of paper clips attached to the tail* for ballast.
Details	Cut out paper helicopters using the dimensions in the diagram below. Bend the wings at about 45 degree angles. Attach one or two paper clips to the tail (making sure they're balanced left to right). Helicopters usually need to be dropped from a height of about 2 m (so a student may need to stand on a chair). Have students record the time from dropping the helicopter to hitting the floor and record the times in a table.	Obtain different weights of paper (you should be able to find different thicknesses of paper around your school). Have students make identical helicopters out of each type of paper. Students should record falling times for each helicopter and enter the data in a table. The table or graph should be constructed with papers from lightest to heaviest listed from left to right on the *x*-axis.	Have your students pick one type or weight of paper and build a paper helicopter. The students should test the falling times for the helicopter with one to five paper clips on the central tail. Students should figure out their own number of replicates, but we find between 5 and 10 is usually sufficient. *Enrichment:* Other modifications such as length of tail are also possible for this study.

FIGURE A2.6

Paper helicopter activity setup

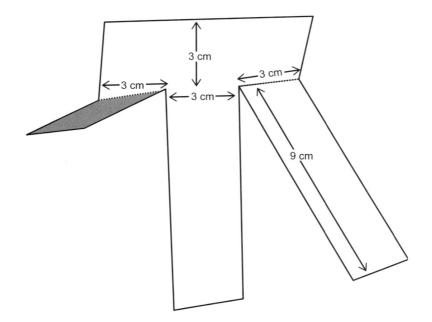

ADDITIONAL NOTES

1. Supplies: Students will need stopwatches.

2. These activities are slightly more abstract than those for which the students mark the data directly on paper because the students have to measure time. (See Figure 2.1, p. 18.)

3. Paper thickness is tricky because there are some very weird (in our view) distinctions that sound similar. If you go shopping at an office store, they can help you find a range of thicknesses to use. A common, and the most accurate, unit for paper thickness is GSM, which means grams per square meter. On the other hand, you can probably figure out by touching it and bending it the order that papers of different thickness would go in.

SOIL MOISTURE AND DISTANCE FROM TREES

Description: This activity has students exploring the factors related to soil moisture and trees. Trees both shade the ground and draw water from it through their roots. The patterns of soil moisture relate to both of those factors. In the following activities, students should measure soil moisture multiple times around the circumference of the tree, record it in a table, and then graph the data appropriately.

	Nominal	Ordinal	Interval-ratio
Overview	Comparing the soil moisture level for two different trees of *similar size but different species* at *x* distance from the trunk.	Comparing the soil moisture level for several trees of the *same species but with different trunk diameters* at *x* distance from the trunk.	Comparing the *soil moisture levels at different distances from the trunk* for a particular tree or tree species.
Details	The overview provides reasonably sufficient detail for collecting the data (each soil moisture meter has its own specific operational instructions). Students need sufficient replicates to feel that the range of possibilities for that test tree has been well represented. There is no hard-and-fast number of replicates that is correct (see Data Literacy Comment 3.2, p. 20).	The overview provides reasonably sufficient detail for collecting the data (each soil moisture meter has its own specific operational instructions). Students need sufficient replicates to feel that the range of possibilities for that test tree has been well represented. There is no hard-and-fast number of replicates that is correct (see Data Literacy Comment 3.2, p. 20).	The overview provides reasonably sufficient detail for collecting the data (each soil moisture meter has its own specific operational instructions). Students need sufficient replicates to feel that the range of possibilities for that test tree has been well represented. There is no hard-and-fast number of replicates that is correct (see Data Literacy Comment 3.2, p. 20).

FIGURE A2.7

Soil moisture activity setup

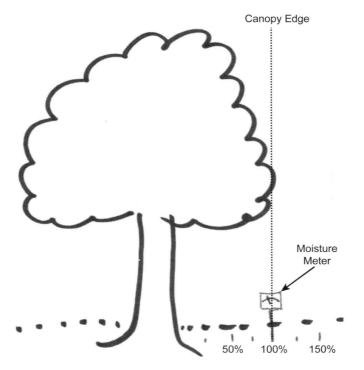

ADDITIONAL NOTES

1. Supplies: Soil moisture meters (available from scientific supply stores, garden stores, or various superstores that have garden centers) and a meter ruler.

2. *x* distance is some proportion of the distance from the trunk to the edge of the tree's canopy. For the nominal category, using the same distance would be acceptable. For ordinal data, it might be a set distance or a proportion of the distance to the edge of the canopy (e.g., halfway from the trunk to the canopy or at the canopy's edge).

3. For the interval-ratio study, the distance is dependent on the size of the tree, but thinking of it proportionally should work. For instance, 25, 50, 75, 100, and 125% of the distance from the trunk to the canopy edge.

HOW FAST DOES IT DISSOLVE?

Description: This activity examines the rates of dissolving of two common (and safe) household materials, sugar and salt, in water. We are looking at the time for a small sample to dissolve. Large unbreakable test tubes such as the Science Kit Baby Soda Bottles (large test tubes with lids) work really well here.

	Nominal	Ordinal	Interval-ratio
Overview	Comparing the *speed of dissolving of sugar and salt*.	Comparing the *speed of dissolving of different forms of sugar*, e.g., fruit sugar (small grains), granulated sugar (medium-size grains), and coarse sugar (large grains).	Comparing *the effect of temperature on how quickly sugar dissolves*. We shall use granulated sugar at a range of temperatures: iced water (≈5°C), cold tap water (≈15°C), hot tap water (≈50°C), mixed equal amounts of cold and hot tap water (≈30°C), and any other combination of hot and cold tap water as needed.
Details	Take two baby soda bottles and pour in some water so that each is the same, about two-thirds full. Add a spoonful of sugar to one, and a spoonful of salt to the other. Replace the lid on each, start the stopwatch, shake both bottles equally, and note the time at which the first one dissolves. Stop the watch when the second sample dissolves.	Take three baby soda bottles and pour in some water so that each is same, about two-thirds full. Add a spoonful of one type of sugar to each bottle. Replace the lids on the bottles, start the stopwatch, and shake the bottles equally. Note the time each sample dissolves. Stop the watch when the third sample dissolves.	You can do this one temperature at a time or all at once. Pour the sample of water into the soda bottle to the line, measure the temperature, add the spoonful of sugar, start timing, and seal the bottle. Shake until dissolved, at which point you stop the timer. Record the result (temperature in degrees Celsius and time in seconds). Repeat for each sample temperature.

ADDITIONAL NOTES

1. Supplies: You will need baby soda bottles (five per group), household salt, regular sugar, fruit (superfine) sugar, coarse sugar, a stopwatch, a thermometer, a teaspoon, and masking tape.

2. These activities are more slightly abstract than those in which the students mark the data directly on paper because the students have to measure time. (See previous page for details.)

3. A cube of sugar has a mass of between 4 g and 5 g. Because we are dissolving comparable amounts in these activities, it is useful to examine how to fill a spoonful of sugar of that mass by weighing several samples.

4. The shaking of each sample needs to be consistent.

5. Baby soda bottles are available at *http://sciencekit.com/baby-soda-bottles/p/IG0034855/*.

EXEMPLARY GRAPH

In the following (Figure A3.1), we identify and detail the factors that contribute to the design of a good graph in a report. We have provided a heading or title; a caption may also be necessary. Jurisdictions vary regarding which is needed, particularly when the graphs are part of a written report (in this case, graphs often have only a caption and not a title). Note that in science reports captions are often more detailed than titles are.

FIGURE A3.1

An exemplary graph

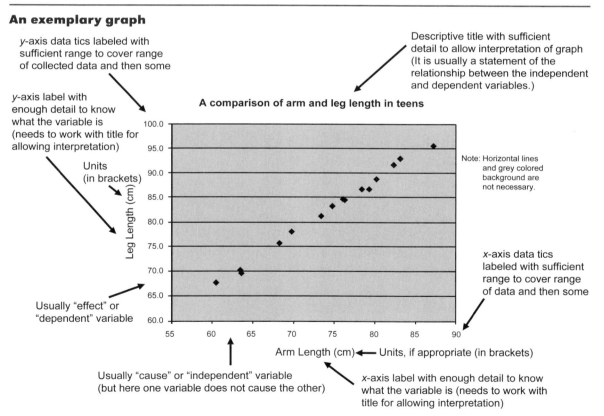

This figure depicts an exemplary graph with labels (in this case one showing an interval-ratio type relationship) so that the reader can learn about the critical parts of a graph. Various jurisdictions may require details other than these; the ones demonstrated here are meant merely as a starting point. Some argue (and some jurisdictions require) that a 0 should be at the bottom left of the graph if one is appropriate (such as here where there is a number line on each axis). If a 0 is required, on either axis, then the number line could be broken to accomplish that with a slash on either side of the gap in the line between the 0 and the next number (as would be appropriate in this example).

EXEMPLARY TABLE

When included in a written report, a good table will have a caption at the top with sufficient description to allow the reader to scan the data in the table and interpret it effectively. Variable names should be labeled, with units if appropriate, as should the general purpose of the columns (usually the treatments, the independent variables) and rows (in our examples, rows are usually replicates or trials). If there are summary statistics at the end of columns (such as mean or median, standard deviation, or total counts, i.e., n), then these should be identified also. For examples of graph design see Chapter 6.

APPENDIX IV
IDEAS FOR EVALUATING LABORATORY REPORTS

Different schools use different types of reporting formats. In general, science laboratory reports have a similarity to the types of articles that scientists write for professional journals, although they usually contain less detail (but some grade 12 students can really surprise you these days).

The general laboratory report contains

- Descriptive Title[1] and Abstract
- Introduction (including a rationale [based on the known science] and a description of what is already known [which scientists would call a literature review])
- Methods section (including step-by-step instructions)
- Data section (with the tables, graphs, and descriptions of the patterns)
- Conclusion and Implications (where the "new" results are tied back to the information that was already known and the implications of that are discussed)

There are, of course, variations on this, such as the vee map report (Appendix V).

Now, we're not going to give you any sort of a marking scheme, but we're going to make some suggestions about how to determine the quality of a laboratory report (which of course will vary by grade level). You'll have to come up with your own way of assigning grades.

SUGGESTIONS FOR REVIEWING A LAB REPORT

Start by asking yourself the following general questions while you read the lab report:

1. What do the researchers (your students) want to find out?

2. Why is it important to investigate or understand this?

3. How are the researchers investigating this? Are their research methods appropriate and adequate to the task?

4. What do they claim to have found out? Are the findings clearly stated? What are the implications of these findings?

---

1. Descriptive titles usually describe the relationship that is being studied. Sometimes the title can be phrased in the form of a question, but in science it is normally a statement. For instance, "What is the relationship between a dog's size and how fast it can run?" is phrasing it in the form of a question. "The relationship between dog size and how fast they can run" is phrasing it in the form of a statement. We are providing a detailed explanation of this here because we find it is the part of laboratory reports that is done most poorly.

GENERAL APPROACH TO REVIEWING A LABORATORY REPORT

1. Read the abstract and introduction for an overview, hypotheses, and conclusions.

2. Carefully review the tables and figures. Draw your own conclusions from them—don't rely on those of the authors of the laboratory report.

3. Read the methods and results section. Make notes on the study design. Do the written results and arguments agree with the tables and figures? Do they agree with your conclusions from step 2?

4. Read the discussion. Do the conclusions follow from the results section? Are there alternative interpretations? Are references used? Have they tried to use any science theories to make sense of their results?

THINGS TO LOOK FOR IN EACH SECTION

TITLE, ABSTRACT, AND INTRODUCTION

- Is the title adequately descriptive of the relationship being studied?
- What are the questions or hypotheses?
- Primary value of the study: new science? technique? novel idea? review?
- Is there an adequate review of previous research or related theory or concepts (however you've defined that for your students)?

METHODS AND RESULTS

- Are the methods clear? Can they be repeated?
- Are diagrams (if needed) sufficient to explain the research approach used? What kinds of evidence are used: descriptive? experimental? both?
- Sampling and experimental design used: Is the sampling random enough? Is there adequate replication? Are the controls appropriate? Are they adequate to test the hypotheses? Would other designs be better?
- Are numbers provided? used in the analyses? used correctly?
- Are tables structured appropriately? Are averages or other summary statistics provided (if appropriate)?
- Are statistics used? Were appropriate statistics used? Are the conclusions from them correct?
- Is data represented using an appropriate graph (or other summary)?

DISCUSSION (ASSUMPTIONS AND INTERPRETATIONS)

- What assumptions are stated? Implied?
- Can these be tested? Should they be?
- Did the investigator seek to support hypotheses or attempt to refute them?
- Is the interpretation supported by all the available data?
- Is there data or a reference for each conclusive statement?
- Is appropriate theory used to support conclusions drawn from the data?
- Do alternatives exist? Are they considered?
- Is the author's interpretation of references correct (if you know)?
- Could the investigator have done better under the circumstances?
- What future studies are suggested by the outcome of this study?

LOOK SPECIFICALLY AT HOW THE DATA ARE REPRESENTED IN TABLES AND GRAPHS

Also see Appendix III.

STRUCTURING TABLES

- Tables usually show raw data with appropriate summary statistics (averages, counts, frequencies, standard deviation, range, and so on).
- Usually, but not always, treatments are in individual columns, different replicates or trials are in the rows.
- Tables are usually structured so that they can be *visually inspected* for patterns in the data *before* the graph is drawn or looked at.

EXAMPLES OF TABLE STRUCTURE

For nominal or ordinal studies, data are usually represented with a bar graph, or in the case of the latter, a line graph (Table A4.1).

TABLE A4.1

An example of a nominal or ordinal study table

	Treatment 1	Treatment 2	Treatment 3	Treatment 4
Replicate 1				
Replicate 2 ...				
Avg.				

Or, for correlational studies, data are usually represented using a scatterplot, sometimes with a trend line (a line of best fit) and a measure of the fit of the line (Table A4.2).

TABLE A4.2

An example of a correlational study table

Variable 1	Variable 2

MAKE SURE STUDENTS HAVE CHOSEN APPROPRIATE GRAPHS

A graph is usually chosen to represent the type of data being collected.

- It is usually appropriate for a bar graph (and, very occasionally, a pie chart) to be used to represent nominal-level data (graphs comparing categories, such as dogs and cats, males and females, Catholics and Protestants and Baptists).

- For ordinal-level data (for which there is an unmeasured but changing category of the same thing, such as small, medium, and large rocks [where those sizes represent a set range; for example, "small" rocks could be classified as 1–3 cm across at the widest point, medium rocks as >3–6 cm across, and "large" rocks as >6 cm across]) it is usually most appropriate to use a line graph, although sometimes a bar graph is appropriate (such as in representing responses to Likert survey questions).

- For interval-ratio-level data (in which both things are measured variables, for instance arm length in cm and leg length in cm), a scatterplot with a trend line is usually most appropriate.

Graphs that have an indicator of the *range of data* in the raw data (either with error bars, or by graphing the raw data and then the averages or lines of best fit [with measures of fit]) are usually better because that allows the reader to better understand how strong the patterns of relationship in the findings are. It is important for an author not to overstate or overemphasize the strength of the patterns in the data.

Note: Both graphs and tables usually have a caption of some sort if they don't have a title. Usually in science reports captions are used instead of titles.

APPENDIX V
CONCEPT MAPS AND VEE MAPS

IDEAS FOR IMPROVING LAB ACTIVITY REPORTING

For teachers unsure about how to start having students report on science investigations, we are providing two previous *Science Scope* articles that outline how to encourage students to work on their ideas about science and develop their own investigations.

THE UNFOLDING VEE

By Wolff-Michael Roth and Michael Bowen

Reprinted with permission from *Science Scope* 16 (5): 28–32.

We will talk about the benefits of using Vee maps to drive those investigations. Like concept maps, Vee maps are less structured than conventional teaching methods. A Vee map guides students through investigations that they choose themselves. This less-structured investigative arrangement allows students to actively learn the principles of investigation.

In following the Vee map, through their investigations, students work to penetrate the structure and meaning of a branch of knowledge. The Vee map helps students to better organize their thinking, investigate more efficiently, and create guidelines for learning. Furthermore, using the Vee map makes students feel better about themselves because they are in control of their own learning and therefore know what they are doing. Figure A5.1 (p. 124) represents our version of the Vee map, a version adapted specifically to suit middle level students.

The left and right sides of the Vee emphasize two interdependent aspects of science learning: knowing and doing, respectively. What students know at any one moment—their existing conceptions, the investigative tools available to them, and their ideas—will determine the quality and quantity of the questions they ask. Conversely, the answers students obtain to their questions will affect what they know, by changing, adding to, refining, or reconfiguring their knowledge. The Vee should lead students to discover the relationship between doing and knowing science. The following six questions lead students through the discovery process, guiding them toward what they need to think about in order to complete their investigation. (Italicized phrases correspond to associated phase names.)

The focus question is "What do I want to find out about?"

"What do I know about the topic?" elicits *associated words*.

"How do I go about finding the answer to my question?" inspires thinking about *investigative activities*.

"What did I observe and measure?" solicits the appropriate *data and data transformations* to provide *meaningful records*.

"What can I make of my findings?" inspires students to make *claims* in terms of the knowledge obtained and its value.

"How do the concepts and events interrelate?" encourages students to construct a *concept map*.

The six guiding questions encourage students to reflect in an orderly manner, providing them with a sort of road map toward new knowledge. Supporting questions to each of the six major headings encourage students to consider the

FIGURE A5.1

An example of a Vee map

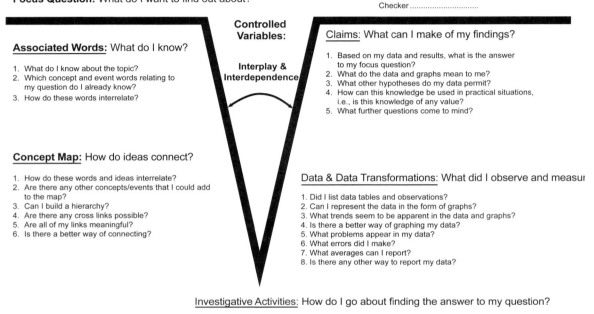

Planning & Reporting My Investigation

Focus Question: What do I want to find out about?

Facilitator.............................
Technician..........................
Recorder.............................
Checker..............................

Associated Words: What do I know?

1. What do I know about the topic?
2. Which concept and event words relating to my question do I already know?
3. How do these words interrelate?

Controlled Variables:

Interplay & Interdependence

Claims: What can I make of my findings?

1. Based on my data and results, what is the answer to my focus question?
2. What do the data and graphs mean to me?
3. What other hypotheses do my data permit?
4. How can this knowledge be used in practical situations, i.e., is this knowledge of any value?
5. What further questions come to mind?

Concept Map: How do ideas connect?

1. How do these words and ideas interrelate?
2. Are there any other concepts/events that I could add to the map?
3. Can I build a hierarchy?
4. Are there any cross links possible?
5. Are all of my links meaningful?
6. Is there a better way of connecting?

Data & Data Transformations: What did I observe and measure

1. Did I list data tables and observations?
2. Can I represent the data in the form of graphs?
3. What trends seem to be apparent in the data and graphs?
4. Is there a better way of graphing my data?
5. What problems appear in my data?
6. What errors did I make?
7. What averages can I report?
8. Is there any other way to report my data?

Investigative Activities: How do I go about finding the answer to my question?

1. How was my investigation set up?
2. What objects/events did I observe?
3. What equipment did I manipulate?
4. What did I use?

questions more specifically in the process of acquiring information to complete their maps.

A MAP FOR LEARNING

The focus question, which drives the investigation, is situated at the top of the Vee. The ability to ask the right kinds of questions and to find the answers to those questions distinguishes scientists from run-of-the-mill thinkers. The focus question "What do I want to find out?" therefore becomes central to an investigation. Before beginning their investigations, it's good for students to ask themselves "What do we know about the topic?" "What experimental techniques are relevant

to the question?" and "How is what I already know interconnected?" as well as to list associated words on the left, or knowing, side of the Vee. These questions inspire students to assess their knowledge before they design and plan their investigations.

The investigative activities take their place beneath the point of the Vee, an appropriate position antithetical to the focus questions, for the bottom of the Vee points to the question "How do I go about finding the answer to my question?" This question focuses on the details of the investigation. To allow student investigations to unfold as in real-life science, students should be allowed to follow contingencies as they develop during the investigation, with intermediary results leading to further focus questions. From this point, the investigation will lead us back up the right side of the Vee.

Under the heading of Data and Data Transformations, students report their observations and provide any maps, data tables, and graphs resulting from the question "What did I observe?" Students should ask themselves such questions as "Did I list all my data and observations?" "Can I represent any of the data in the form of graphs?" "Is there any better way of graphing my data?" and so forth to complete this work.

Next, students formulate claims from their data and graphs; for example, they should ask themselves "What can I make of my findings?" Resulting claims should not be restricted to simple factual statements. All knowledge, in some way, has implications for society at large. Students may even need to do research to find out what these implications are. For example, students should consider ways the information can be put to use in practical situations and the value of their newly obtained knowledge. Afterward, students investigate the doing side of the investigation or right side of the Vee and reflect on what they learned.

Creating a relevant concept map encourages students to reflect on vocabulary-building words they've encountered during the activity and how these different words are interconnected. Because a concept map reflects students' current level of knowledge, it is located on the left side of the Vee. Students can increase their productivity in this task by asking themselves such questions as "Are there any other concepts/investigative activities that we can add?" "Are there any possible cross-links between different parts of the concept map?" and "Is there a better way of connecting our words or concepts." …

The Vee map in [Figure A5.2, p. 126] was prepared by a group of students during [an] eight-week open-inquiry unit on biomes. [It] shows how sophisticated investigations can become when students are given the freedom to frame their own questions. Following self-planned research agendas stimulated students' interest in related courses, increased their motivation to find out on their own, and encouraged them to link their classroom experience to the real world outside of school.

EVALUATING STUDENT WORK

At Appleby College, a prep school, students in grades six through ten work on individual projects throughout the year for their science classes. As with most types of assignments that teachers must evaluate, there are different ways of scoring Vee maps. Figure A5.3 (p. 127) shows a scoring scheme that has worked for Appleby faculty in the past, but the weights given to each of the areas on the Vee map are arbitrary and can be changed to fit individual needs. For example, when the teacher gives a focus question at the beginning of a unit to get students started, less weight may be assigned to this part. On the other hand, given that the data and data transformations, claims, and concept map take more time and intellectual effort, we like to weight them more heavily.

For teachers who like to give marks as percentage points, the following grading system is a possible suggestion. Weight the areas of concept map, data and data transformation, and claims twice as heavily as associated words and investigative activities, yielding 24 points (6, 6, 6, 3, and 3) for a perfect map. If you include one point for overall outlook and presentation, then multiplying a student's score by 4 would yield a percentage score. Using a chart like that in Figure A5.4 (p. 127), a student's progress can be monitored for each of the areas of the Vee

FIGURE A5.2

A Vee map created during an eight-week inquiry unit on biomes

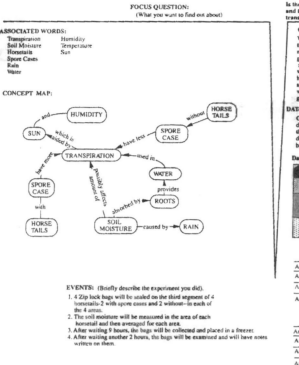

FOCUS QUESTION:
(What you want to find out about)

ASSOCIATED WORDS:
Transpiration   Humidity
Soil Moisture   Temperature
Horsetails   Sun
Spore Cases
Rain
Water

CONCEPT MAP:

EVENTS: (Briefly describe the experiment you did).
1. 4 Zip lock bags will be sealed on the third segment of 4 horsetails–2 with spore cases and 2 without–in each of the 4 areas.
2. The soil moisture will be measured in the area of each horsetail and then averaged for each area.
3. After waiting 9 hours, the bags will be collected and placed in a freezer.
4. After waiting another 2 hours, the bags will be examined and will have notes written on them.

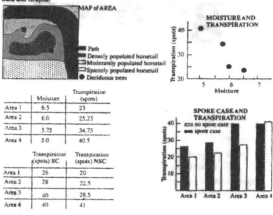

Is there a relationship between the amount of transpiration of horse tails and the soil moisture? Is there a difference between the amount of transpiration of horse tails with and without spore cases?

CLAIMS

We found that areas with the least amount of moisture tend to have more transpiration than those with more moisture. This could be that all the areas received the same amount of moisture but some of the areas with less moisture (Area 2 and Area 3) have horsetails which grow more densely together therefore all the water would be absorbed more quickly than areas with sparse growth (Area 1). In the case of Area 4 which is located on an eroded slope, all the water which it receives runs down the slope and into the creek. Therefore the roots of these horsetails absorb the water as quickly as possible. In all cases except for one, horsetails with spore cases transpired more than horsetails without spore cases. This could be that horsetails with spore cases produce more cells and therefore more photosynthesis occurs and there is a greater exchange of gases and more oxygen and water vapour is released.

DATA & TRANSFORMATIONS:

Observations: Initially, the amount of transpiration of the horsetails was very low and hard to distinguish from one another, i.e., make comparisons and conclusions. After placing the bags in the freezer, it appeared that the water vapour had frozen into little ice particles about 1 mm in diameter. Finding no other way, we counted the white spots in each bag and used that as the basis to judge the amount of transpiration.

Data and Graphs:

MAP of AREA
■ Path
▣ Densely populated horsetail
▨ Moderately populated horsetail
▢ Sparsely populated horsetail
● Deciduous trees

MOISTURE AND TRANSPIRATION

SPORE CASE AND TRANSPIRATION

	Moisture	Transpiration (spots)
Area 1	6.5	23
Area 2	6.0	25.25
Area 3	5.75	34.75
Area 4	5.0	40.5

	Transpiration (spots) SC	Transpiration (spots) NSC
Area 1	26	20
Area 2	28	22.5
Area 3	40	28.5
Area 4	40	41

map over the period of a term, or possibly even an entire year.

In spite of concerns about rigid assessment practices and the practice of assigning value to students' work in the form of letter grades, teachers must not forget that all assessment necessarily requires some judgment and thus contains elements of subjectivity. We have found, as have others before us, that in general there is good agreement among scorers of Vee maps (Novak and Gowin 1984). However, so many alternatives exist for constructing a concept map on a given topic that we must remain flexible in scoring to do justice to a student's learning style and way of expression. Over time, after scoring several sets of Vee maps, one can develop a set of criteria to consistently and quickly evaluate an entire class of students work. When students work in groups of two to three students, the actual number of Vee maps marked is much smaller than number of students. In these situations, students indicate on the top right-hand side of the Vee the individual roles they will be taking or have taken during a Vee-map-directed investigation.

Novak, J., and D. Gowin. 1984. *Learning how to learn*. Cambridge, England: Cambridge University Press.

FIGURE A5.3

Scoring scheme for Vee-map assignments

Name:

Focus Question	Events/Objects	Concepts/Concept map (times 2)	Data & Transformation (times 2)	Claims (times 2)	Comments: _____
					0 - The area on the Vee Map is not indentified, or does not contain any information
					1 - The area is indentified, but there are inconsistencies with other areas on the map.
					2 - The area is indentified and no inconsistencies exist; good representation of the new knowledge in map
					3 - The area is identified, no inconsistencies exist, and additional suggestions, links, questions, data, transformations exist

FIGURE A5.4

A chart for keeping track of students' progress in using the Vee map

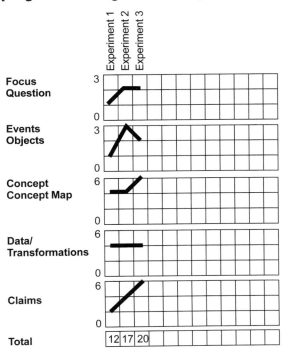

MAPS FOR MORE MEANINGFUL LEARNING

By Wolff-Michael Roth and Michael Bowen

Reprinted with permission from *Science Scope* 16 (4): 24–25.

In real life, problems are quite often messy, poorly defined, and call for creative problem solving. To solve problems, people actively interact with their environment, learning as they go along and using knowledge from past experience (Knorr-Cetina 1983). School learning is often antithetical to real life, creating situations in which students perceive themselves as passive, with neither control over the problems nor choice in selecting problem-solving processes (Lave 1988). The discrepancy between real life and school learning negatively affects students' performance and attitudes (Bereiter 1985).

GIVING STUDENTS CONTROL

At Appleby College, a preparatory school where I formerly taught in Oakville, Ontario, Canada, faculty approach curriculum development and teaching progressively. They make science more relevant to everyday life, so the teaching–learning context becomes more like an apprenticeship for joining a community of practicing scientists. Thus, the faculty provides students with a context that allows students to frame their own questions and answer the questions through investigations. In this open-inquiry process, teachers help students to construct conceptual frameworks for knowledge and acquire new practical and analytical skills.

At other times, students design experiments to investigate questions to which the teachers do not know the answers. In such cases, teachers engage students in the inquiry, make suggestions that the students may or may not follow, and propose hypotheses for students to investigate along with their own.

Teachers demonstrate the use of science skills and coach students to new levels of proficiency in using inquiry skills to research problems of genuine interest to them. Students are truly interested in their research because they choose their own research topics.

Faculty at Appleby College encourage students to learn meaningfully in an open-inquiry format using two teaching–learning heuristics, the concept map and the Vee map (Novak and Gowin 1984). In this article, we focus primarily on concept mapping. …

INTRODUCING CONCEPT MAPS

Concept mapping was designed to assist learners in understanding concepts and relationships between them, to establish hierarchical relationships among concepts, and to recognize the evolving nature of scientific understanding. When teaching students to use concept maps, have students map the key concepts from an assigned reading or their findings from a laboratory investigation. Figure A5.5 shows a concept map prepared by two eighth-grade students who had just completed an investigation that was part of an eight-week open-inquiry unit on biomes in the school's backyard. The two students had chosen a plot of land on the school grounds and designed an investigation to answer the question, "What type of soil porosity, texture, compounds, and color are there in our plot?"

Have students work in groups on their concept maps. First, give them slips of paper on which to write the concepts they would like to map. It's easy for students to move around slips of paper, maneuvering them so that associated concepts are near one another. By working in groups, students tend to discuss the material they're mapping, which helps them to clarify the meanings and relationships between the concepts. After students have their concepts well placed, they copy down the positions of the concepts onto notebook paper and then draw connecting lines to show interrelationships. Students draw the connecting lines as arrows and label each with the name of the relationship it describes.

Our studies found that working on concept maps forces students to truly understand information of which they only have an intuitive understanding or understand only through mathematical reasoning. Forcing students to articulate their own ideas in their own words helps students recognize the gaps in their understanding. The concept-mapping process gets students to reexamine their ideas and consider them in the context of the initial experiment, and to try to connect new ideas to each other and to their prior knowledge. When designing concept maps, students frequently realize that they don't really know how ideas are related, leading them to develop new questions to investigate. Also, research shows that

FIGURE A5.5

A concept map prepared by two eighth-grade students completing a unit on biomes

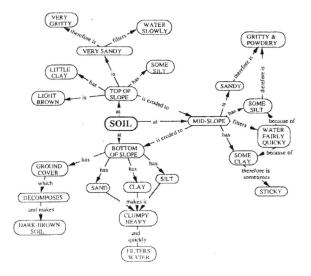

REFERENCES

Bereiter, C. 1985. Toward a solution of the learning paradox. *Review of Educational Research* 55 (2): 201–225.

Jegede, O. J., E. E. Alaiyemola, and P. A. Okebukola. 1990. The effect of concept mapping on students' anxiety in biology. *Journal of Research in Science Teaching* 27 (10): 951–960.

Knorr-Cetina, K. D. 1983. Toward a constructivist interpretation of science. In *Science observed: Perspectives on the social study of science*, ed. K. D. Knorr-Cetina and M. Mulkay. London: Sage Publications.

Lave, J. 1988. *Cognition in practice*. Cambridge, England: Cambridge University Press.

Novak, J. D., and D. B. Gowin. 1984. *Learning how to learn*. Cambridge, England: Cambridge University Press.

group work on concept mapping may reduce students' anxiety (Jegede, Alaiyemola, and Okebukola 1990).

PASSIVE TEACHERS, ACTIVE LEARNERS

Often we, as teachers, let students develop an intuitive understanding on their own and later provide them with the terminology with which to express their ideas. In contrast to this more conventional learning-cycle approach, concept mapping is less structured. Students learn at their own pace—in much the same way as shop apprentices—receiving individual assistance as they or their teacher perceives the need for it.

APPENDIX VI
WEB RESOURCES

1. A manual from the Harvard Forest Schoolyard Science Program

http://harvardforest.fas.harvard.edu/sites/harvardforest.fas.harvard.edu/files/publications/pdfs/Colburn_Schoolyard%20Graphing%20Manual_2009.pdf

This is a complete manual for school-based field biology with a strong focus on graphing.

Publication details: Colburn, B. A. 2009. *Show Me a Picture, Tell Me a Story: An Introduction to Graphs for the Analysis of Ecological Data from Schoolyard Science Research Studies*. Harvard Forest Schoolyard Science Program, Harvard Forest, Harvard University, Petersham, MA.

2. The website *Biology4all*

This U.K.-based site has links to four web pages with downloadable Excel worksheets for International Baccalaureate–level biology:

Statistics: *www.biology4all.com/resources_library/details.asp?ResourceID=63*

Statistics, kite charts in Excel: *www.biology4all.com/resources_library/details.asp?ResourceID=159*

Statistics, box plots in Excel: *www.biology4all.com/resources_library/details.asp?ResourceID=163*

Statistics for AS- and A2-level biology: *www.biology4all.com/resources_library/details.asp?ResourceID=62*

3. *The Open Door Web Site*: Measurements Chapters Index

www.saburchill.com/physics/chap03.html

This page has the following sections:

- Making measurements
- Graphs
- Digital measuring instruments
- Experimental reports

4. Tables and Graphs by Chris Joyce, Alex Neill, Verena Watson, Jonathan Fisher

http://arb.nzcer.org.nz/supportmaterials/tables.php

This page is part of the New Zealand Council for Educational Research Assessment Resource Banks. Intended for teachers' self-directed professional development, it contains the following sections:

- What are tables and graphs?
- Why do we want students to know about tables and graphs?
- What are the problem areas for students?
- Variables—what are they?
- Constructing tables
- Constructing graphs

- Interpreting tables and graphs
- Implications for teaching
- Possible progressions in teaching about graphs

5. Graphs: Student Misconceptions and Strategies for Teaching
   www.epcae.org/uploads/documents/Graphs_Sept%2020.pdf
   From The El Paso Collaborative for Academic Excellence, the Consortium for Policy Research in Education, and The Consortium for the Advancement of Mathematics and Science. The authors' description is, "This paper summarizes some of the research into students' difficulties understanding graphs and the connections between graphs, data sets, functions, and real-world situations."

6. Data and Graphs on *Science-class.net*
   http://science-class.net/NOS/data_graphs.htm
   Set at grades 5 to 9, this page has links to other graphing activities.

7. *The Open Door Web Site*: All About Graphs
   www.saburchill.com/IBbiology/graphs/001.html
   Aimed at students in International Baccalaureate biology, this page reaffirms the message in this book, but also offers guidance in the use of MS Excel.

   - Graphs, why use them?
   - Rules for drawing graphs
   - Graph drawing with MS Excel
   - Other types of graphical representation

8. The National Center for Education Statistics (NCES) Kids' Zone: Create a Graph
   http://nces.ed.gov/nceskids/createagraph/default.aspx
   This is an online graphing portal. It will create five types of graph: bar, line, area, pie or *x-y*. Students and teachers can enter their own data.
   The page contains a link to an online graphing tutorial:
   http://nces.ed.gov/nceskids/help/user_guide/graph/index.asp

9. Using Graphs and Visual Data in Science by Anne Egger, PhD, Anthony Carpi, PhD (2008).
   www.visionlearning.com/en/library/Process-of-Science/49/Data:-Using-Graphs-and-Visual-Data/156
   This is an overview piece covering the introduction to the use of graphs in the 18th century to the political use of graphs in the 21st century. The authors use the following:

   - Using graphs to present numerical data
   - Interpreting graphs
   - Error and uncertainty estimation in visual data
   - Misuse of scientific images
   - Visualizing spatial and three-dimensional data

- Working with image-based data
- Graphs for scientific communication

10. Statistics Canada: Line graphs

www.statcan.gc.ca/edu/power-pouvoir/ch9/line-lineaire/5214824-eng.htm

This page from the Canadian government statistics unit sets out four features of line graphs:

- Plotting a trend over time
- Comparing two related variables
- Using correct scale
- Multiple line graphs

11. Critical insights on graphing

For the Love of Graphs, ABC Science Opinion by Paul Willis: *www.abc.net.au/science/articles/2013/04/29/3740590.htm*

The statisticians at Fox News use classic and novel graphical techniques to lead with data, by Jeff Leek: *http://simplystatistics.org/2012/11/26/the-statisticians-at-fox-news-use-classic-and-novel-graphical-techniques-to-lead-with-data/*

The first site is a critical discussion of how graphs can mislead as much as they can inform. The second site gives examples of how an American news station presents statistics in a way to misrepresent what the graphs actually mean.

12. Discussion of *t*-tests

http://archive.bio.ed.ac.uk/jdeacon/statistics/tress4a.html

This archived page provides discussions of:

- What a *t*-test is
- Provides a worked-out example of a *t*-test
- *t*-tests conducted by Microsoft Excel
- How to interpret *t*-tests in publications

13. *t*-Test calculators

http://ncalculators.com/statistics/t-test-calculator.htm

This page provides a calculator to work out a *t*-test.

Determination of the statistical significance of the calculated *t*-statistic needs to consult a critical value table such as that at *http://archive.bio.ed.ac.uk/jdeacon/statistics/table1.html#Student's t test* or *http://easycalculation.com/statistics/t-distribution-critical-value-table.php*

14. Discussion of correlation and regression analysis

http://archive.bio.ed.ac.uk/jdeacon/statistics/tress11.html#Correlation coefficient

This page provides a discussion of how to calculate a correlation and a regression analysis using example data and provided formulas. In addition, it demonstrates how to use an analysis of variance

(ANOVA) to calculate the significance of a line fitted to a data set. An example using Microsoft Excel is also provided, and there is a discussion of how to deal with data that has a nonlinear pattern.

15. *r*-Squared calculators

http://easycalculation.com/statistics/r-squared.php

http://ncalculators.com/statistics/r-squared-calculator.htm

These two online calculators can determine the *r*-squared value, which indicates how well a line of best fit fits the data. The second link provides a detailed description of what an *r*-squared value represents.

16. Bar charts and histograms

http://stattrek.com/statistics/charts/histogram.aspx

http://mathcentral.uregina.ca/QQ/database/QQ.09.99/raeluck1.html

These pages discuss the distinction between bar charts and histograms and provide examples. Histograms are sometimes used in science instead of other types of graphs when there is continuous data.

17. Statistical calculators

www.graphpad.com/quickcalcs/

A collection of simple on-line calculators and analysis tools for both categorical (nominal and ordinal) and continuous (interval-ratio) data, including *t*-tests, *F*-tests and chi-square analysis.

18. Discussions of ANOVA

   i.   *http://udel.edu/~mcdonald/statanovaintro.html*

   ii.   *http://udel.edu/~mcdonald/statanovasig.html*

   iii.   *www.physics.csbsju.edu/stats/anova.html*

   iv.   *http://easycalculation.com/statistics/one-way-anova-matrix.php*

   v.   *http://easycalculation.com/statistics/one-way-anova.php*

   vi.   *www.itl.nist.gov/div898/handbook/eda/section3/eda3673.htm*

An introduction to one-way ANOVA tests, with further links to provide more detail and a worked-out example. The third site provides both a description of an ANOVA and an online calculator tool. The fourth and fifth links provide an online calculator tool. The sixth site is the critical value table for ANOVA analysis.

APPENDIX VII
AN INTRODUCTION TO DATA MANAGEMENT FROM A MATHEMATICS PERSPECTIVE

By Eva Knoll

Mathematics Education, Mount Saint Vincent University, Halifax, Nova Scotia

Data management is the most concrete branch of mathematics because it applies to a particular context—it is used to analyze a specific situation. It is a great candidate for cross-curricular teaching because it can easily be applied to other subjects such as language arts, social studies, economics, science, and so on.

There are six basic questions, or steps, in data management:

1. What are you trying to find out?

2. What are you trying to represent?

3. What are you expecting to see?

4. How would you represent this result?

5. What does the result show?

6. Is your representation a useful one?

WHAT ARE YOU TRYING TO FIND OUT?

The purpose of data management activities is to find out something about the world. The first step is to figure out what it is that the data management activity is meant to determine. In other words, what question will it answer? The other steps all emerge from the answer to this one. This is also where the data collection instrument is developed and applied.

WHAT ARE YOU TRYING TO REPRESENT?

On the basis of the previous step, the data manager decides what the answer to the question could look like. Is the answer a single, significant value, such as an average or a maximum value, or is it a distribution, a tendency, a change over time (or lack thereof)?

This step focuses on deciding which of the following values or displays will help answer the question posed:

- Significant values
    - minimum value, maximum value
    - range of values (calculated as max-min)
    - mean
    - median
    - mode
- Other tendencies
    - distribution and frequency of values
    - proportion of the data set with specific values or groups (intervals) of values
    - correlations between variables
    - change over time or against another variable

WHAT ARE YOU EXPECTING TO SEE?

This step is critical. A data manager always, consciously or unconsciously, has a sense of what the outcome is likely to be. Making this expectation explicit by articulating and then verifying a prediction will increase the impact of the findings. An unexpected result will prompt reflections about why there is a discrepancy with the prediction: Was there an error in the process (in which case the prediction might still be more accurate than the "result")? a factor that was not considered (in which case the process was sound but the prediction skewed by a bias or lack of information about the context)? or both? A result that was predicted is an insight as well.

- For each isolated or calculated value and for the other tendencies you are determining from your data, what do you expect to see?
- This step will give you insight into how to represent the results (step 4).
- Make note of the prediction and be as specific as you can so you will later be able to verify your prediction (step 5). This will give you the *full impact* of the result.

HOW WOULD YOU REPRESENT THIS RESULT?

This step is linked to steps 2 and 3. The decision is made as to the most effective way to represent the salient value or tendency so it can be picked out, examined, and interpreted.

- Note that charts are *not* interchangeable: different charts show different things in different ways
- Selecting a chart or special value depends on the following:
  - o type of variables
  - o type of data
  - o what you want to show, compare, or contrast
  - o the amount of detail
  - o the type of relationship

WHAT DOES THE RESULT SHOW?

This is the interpretation step. What did the value/chart that was calculated or constructed show? How do the results compare to the prediction(s) made in step 3?

- Link back and compare to the prediction
- Skills similar to those of step 3
- Is the chart/value showing what you predicted?
  - o If yes, what is this telling you?
  - o If no, what is this telling you? Why might that be?

DOES IT TELL YOU WHAT YOU WANT TO KNOW?

This step focuses on the result and links it back to the question. It is the reflective "looking-back" step. Did the process answer the question it was meant to? Would a different data collection method, a different chart, or a different calculation have been more helpful? This is the step where real learning takes place.

The six questions are designed to incite reflection at the crucial steps of data management activities. The questions are each designed to reframe thinking at the various stages of the process. Each is essential in a normal process. In a learning context, depending on the intended learning outcomes, some of the steps can be prepared in advance by the instructor. However, it is important to discuss the steps with the students. Even if the chart is provided (i.e., no data collection is done by the students), it is useful to spend some time discussing what would be a good way to collect data (step 2) based on what the question is (step 1). A well-structured guided-discovery lesson can lead the class in the right direction while remaining student centered.

Note the following:

- The steps are not all answered by learners at every grade. Instead, they are the *aim* of the teaching of data management.
- When you prepare activities for the classroom, isolate the step or steps that you are teaching and *complete the others yourself in the activity preparation.*

EXAMPLE

For example, if you are teaching about *reading a picture graph*, you will prepare the graph yourself (or check that an existing graph from another source is good per steps 2 and 4), formulate the questions (step 1), and let your students work on steps 3, 5, and 6.

3. What are you expecting to see?

This is an important step: You are articulating your expectations, and this will guide you in *interpreting* the results you do obtain. Ask the students to predict what the chart will look like before you give it to them.

5. What does the result show?

This step links back to the predictions that were made in step 3. As such, they are the connection of the math to the context of the activity. This is when the charts and special values are interpreted.

6. Is your representation a useful one?

This step is the most conceptual and the one that focuses a critical look at the process as a whole. It is a look back at the whole process, particularly step 4, with an evaluative eye. This is where the learning is the richest.

- It is important, however, that the children get a chance to *decide for themselves* what would be appropriate.
    - o variables to consider
    - o questions to ask
    - o charts to build and values to calculate

This gives students the opportunity to take ownership of their understanding.

APPENDIX VIII
t-TEST OF EXAMPLE DATA

I n examining the data comparisons between Figures 1.6 and 1.7 (p. 10) readers might have some doubt that the images would be statistically significant in one case and not in the other. The graphs were not derived from real data (although the patterns are similar to those from those sorts of studies). However, that isn't relevant because the distance of each dot from the baseline will suffice. So, the data from Figure 1.6 was measured (using a ruler) and data tables constructed. A similar data set was then constructed for Figure 1.7 (but with the same number of data points as Figure 1.6, falling within the data ranges around the means in Figure 1.7—the number of data points was kept the same so that it was removed as something that the reader thought might be influencing the *t*-values, and repeating values were chosen to obtain the same mean). A *t*-test was then conducted to compare the means on each graph (Figure A8.1, p. 140).

FIGURE A8.1

The overlapping data from Figures 1.6 and 1.7

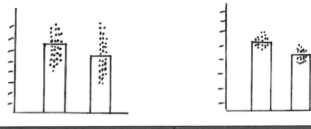

	Figure 1.6 (wide distribution)				Figure 1.7 (narrow distribution)			
	Group 1		Group 2		Group 1		Group 2	
	3.6	2.6	3	3.7	2.8	3.45	2.5	3.05
	3.8	2.4	3.3	2.7	2.85	3.55	2.5	3.15
	4	3.3	3.5	2.5	2.95	3.9	2.6	3.5
	4.2	3.2	3.8	1.9	3	3.85	2.7	3.4
	3.6	2.8	4.1	1.6	3.05	3.5	2.8	3.1
	3.9	2.6	4.3	2.8	3.2	3.8	2.9	3.4
	4.1	2.3	3.1	2.6	3.45	3.7	3.15	3.3
	4.3	2.1	3.3	2.4	2.85	3.8	2.5	3.4
	3.6	3.2	3.5	2.2	2.85	3.5	2.55	3.3
	3.9	3.0	3.8	2.0	2.95	3.45	2.65	3.2
	4.1	2.6	4.0	1.8	3	3.3	2.7	3.1
	3.6	3.3	4.3	1.5	3.1	3.35	2.8	3.1
	3.9	3.2	4.6	2.7	3.05	3.35	2.75	3.1
	3.3	2.8	3.1	2.5	3.2	3.4	2.9	3.2
	3.1	2.6	3.3	2.2	3.1	3.45	2.8	3.3
	2.9		3.5	2.0	3.15		2.85	3.35
Avg.	3.287097		2.9875		3.287097		2.9875	
n	31		32		31		32	
SD	0.614		0.849		0.3212		0.3072	
SEM	0.11		0.15		0.0577		0.0543	
t-Statistic	1.6011				3.7844*			
Degrees of freedom	61				61			
SED	0.187				0.079			

SD = standard deviation; SED = standard error of difference; SEM = standard error of the mean.

*Means are statistically significant since the value is greater than the content value of 2.04 (see Table 8.1, p. 52). Significance is due to the narrow data scatter and the minimal overlap of the data. This is quantitatively apparent by the lower standard deviation than that found in Figure 2.5.

As can be seen, the graph with overlapping raw data (Figure 1.6, p. 10) did not have means that were statistically different from each other, whereas the graph (Figure 1.7, p. 10) with little overlapping data *did* have means that were significantly different. As this demonstrates, teaching students about graphing raw data and taking variation into consideration when drawing conclusions from the graphs *does* better approximate the practices of scientists in working with data.

APPENDIX IX
WORKSHEETS FOR STATISTICAL ANALYSIS

I n our experience, most student inquiry investigations can be analyzed using one of three statistical approaches: a *t*-test, an analysis of variance (ANOVA) test (which can also require some post hoc (i.e., "after") analysis), or a regression and correlation analysis.

In this appendix, we have provided worksheets so that upper-level students can try their hand at these sorts of statistical analyses. There are, of course, any number of programs[1] that could churn out these numbers for you quite quickly (see Appendix VI), but we believe there is some benefit in playing with the analyses by hand first.

We have also provided a worked-out example (using data from various chapters in the book) using these worksheets, so that if students get stuck on analyzing their own data they can look at a worked-through example using the same worksheets.

---

1. Current plans are for NSTA Press to host web pages that will allow this analysis to be done online. Other worksheets for other statistical analyses will also be released at this site as they are developed.

t-TEST WORKSHEET

	Group 1: _____		Group 2: _____	
	(a)	(a) × (a)	(b)	(b) × (b)
1				
2				
3				
4				
5				
6				
7				
8				
9				
10				
11				
12				
13				
14				
15				
Sum	(c)	(d)	(e)	(f)
Count	(g)		(h)	

Step 1: Enter data in table in rows (a) and (b).

Step 2: Square (a) and put in column (a) × (a); square (b) and put in column (b) × (b).

Step 3: Sum columns (a), (a) × (a), (b) and (b) × (b) and put results on Sum row.

Step 4: Count measures in column (a) and (b) and enter them on the Count row.

Step 5: Calculate: $\dfrac{(c) \times (c)}{(g)}$ = _____ (i) $\dfrac{(e) \times (e)}{(h)}$ = _____ (j)

Step 6: Calculate: (d) − (i) = _____ (k)   (f) − (j) = _____ (l)

Step 7: Calculate: (k) + (l) = _____ (m)

Step 8: Calculate: $\dfrac{(m)}{(g) + (h) - 2}$ = _____ (n)

Step 9: Calculate: $(n) \times \left(\dfrac{(1)}{(g)} + \dfrac{(1)}{(h)} \right)$ = (n) × (_____ + _____) = _____ (o)

Step 10: Calculate: $\sqrt{(o)}$ = _____ (p)

Step 11: Calculate: $\dfrac{(c)}{(g)}$ = _____ (q) $\dfrac{(e)}{(h)}$ = _____ (r)

Step 12: Calculate: (q) – (r) = | _____ | (s) (Note: Absolute value of [s])

Step 13: Calculate: t-statistic = $\dfrac{(s)}{(p)}$ = _____

Step 14: Calculate: degrees of freedom (d.f.) = (g) + (h) – 2 = _____

5% Significance Table			
Degrees of freedom	Critical value	Degrees of freedom	Critical value
4	2.78	15	2.13
5	2.57	16	2.12
6	2.48	18	2.10
7	2.37	20	2.09
8	2.31	22	2.07
9	2.26	24	2.06
10	2.23	26	2.06
11	2.20	28	2.05
12	2.18	30	2.04
13	2.16	40	2.02
14	2.15	60	2.00
		120	1.98

You must now compare your calculated t-statistic to the appropriate value in the significance table. Find the table value beside the appropriate degrees of freedom and enter it below.

Critical value: _____

Calculated t-statistic: _____

If the t-statistic you calculated is *less than* the critical value in the table above (for the correct degrees of freedom), then the difference between the two means is nonsignificant. This indicates that there is statistically *no difference* between the Group 1 and Group 2 data.

If the calculated t-statistic is *greater than* the critical value in the table above (for the correct degrees of freedom), then the difference between the two means is statistically *significant.* This indicates that *there is a statistical difference* between the Group 1 and Group 2 data.

Check the appropriate box:

Significant ☐   Nonsignificant ☐

Assumptions for this test to be valid:

1. The samples were chosen randomly.

2. The data scatter about the means is more-or-less the same "width" for both groups (meaning the standard deviations are similar).

3. The data is more close to the means and less away from the means (a "normal" distribution).

4. The data in Group 1 come from a different group than those in Group 2 (they're not repeated measures on the same individuals or samples—there's a special *t*-test for that).

WORKED-OUT *t*-TEST WORKSHEET

(Using the dog and cat data from Table 3.1, p. 19.)

	Group 1: Dogs sleeping		Group 2: Cats sleeping	
	(a)	(a) × (a)	(b)	(b) × (b)
1	8	64	14	196
2	9	81	5	25
3	5	25	7	7
4	8	64	8	8
5	7	49	7	7
6				
7				
8				
9				
10				
11				
12				
13				
14				
15				
Sum	37 (c)	283 (d)	41 (e)	383 (f)
Count	5 (g)		5 (h)	

Step 1: Enter data in table in rows (a) and (b).

Step 2: Square (a) and put in column (a) × (a); square (b) and put in column (b) × (b).

Step 3: Sum columns (a), (a) × (a), (b) and (b) × (b) and put results on Sum row.

Step 4: Count measures in column (a) and (b) and enter them on the Count row.

Step 5: Calculate: $\dfrac{(c) \times (c)}{(g)}$ = __273.8__ (i) $\dfrac{(e) \times (e)}{(h)}$ = __336.2__ (j)

Step 6: Calculate: (d) − (i) = __9.2__ (k) (f) − (j) = __46.8__ (l)

Step 7: Calculate: (k) + (l) = __56__ (m)

Step 8: Calculate: $\dfrac{\overline{(m)}}{(g) + (h) - 2}$ = ___7___ (n)

Step 9: Calculate: $(n) \times \left(\dfrac{(1)}{(g)} + \dfrac{(1)}{(h)} \right)$ = (n) × (___0.2___ + ___0.2___) = ___2.8___ (o)

Step 10: Calculate: $\sqrt{(o)}$ = ___1.67332___ (p)

Step 11: Calculate: $\dfrac{\overline{(c)}}{(g)}$ = ___7.4___ (q) $\dfrac{(e)}{(h)}$ = ___8.2___ (r)

Step 12: Calculate: (q) – (r) = | ___0.8___ | (s) (Note: Absolute value of [s])

Step 13: Calculate: t-statistic = $\dfrac{(s)}{(p)}$ = ___0.478___

Step 14: Calculate: degrees of freedom (d.f.) = (g) + (h) – 2 = ___8___

5% Significance Table			
Degrees of freedom	Critical value	Degrees of freedom	Critical value
4	2.78	15	2.13
5	2.57	16	2.12
6	2.48	18	2.10
7	2.37	20	2.09
8	2.31	22	2.07
9	2.26	24	2.06
10	2.23	26	2.06
11	2.20	28	2.05
12	2.18	30	2.04
13	2.16	40	2.02
14	2.15	60	2.00
		120	1.98

You must now compare your calculated t-statistic to the appropriate value in the significance table. Find the table value beside the appropriate degrees of freedom and enter it below.

Critical value: ___2.31___

Calculated t-statistic: ___0.478___

If the t-statistic you calculated is *less than* the critical value in the table above (for the correct degrees of freedom), then the difference between the two means is *nonsignificant*. This indicates that there is statistically *no difference* between the Group 1 and Group 2 data.

If the calculated t-statistic is *greater than* the critical value in the table above (for the correct degrees of freedom), then the difference between the two means is statistically *significant*. This indicates that *there is a statistical difference* between the Group 1 and Group 2 data.

Check the appropriate box:

Significant ☐   Nonsignificant ☒

ANOVA WORKSHEET

(More than two comparison groups or treatments.)

	Treatment 1: _____		Treatment 2: _____		Treatment 3: _____		Treatment 4: _____	
1	(a)	(a) × (a)	(b)	(b) × (b)	(c)	(c) × (c)	(d)	(d) × (d)
2								
3								
4								
5								
6								
7								
8								
9								
10								
11								
12								
13								
14								
15								
Sum	(c)	(d)	(e)	(f)	(g)	(h)	(i)	(j)
Count	(k)		(l)		(m)		(n)	

Step 1: Enter data in rows (a) through (d) (assuming four different treatments or observation categories; more may be added).

Step 2: Square values in each of (a) through (d), and put in column immediately to the right.

Step 3: Sum each column, and put results on Sum row.

Step 4: Count measures in each column (a) through (d), and enter them on the Count row.

Step 5: Calculate full table values:

Total sum: (c) + (e) + (g) + (i) = _____ (o)

Total sum of squared numbers: (d) + (f) + (h) + (j) = _____ (p)

Total Count: (k) + (l) + (m) + (n) = _____ (q)

Step 6: Calculate *correction term*: (o) × $\frac{(o)}{(q)}$ = _____ (r)

Step 7: Calculate *sum of squares total* (SSt): (p) − (r) = _____ (s)

Step 8: Calculate: $\dfrac{(c) \times (c)}{(k)} + \dfrac{(e) \times (e)}{(l)} + \dfrac{(g) \times (g)}{(m)} + \dfrac{(i) \times (i)}{(n)}$ = _____ (t)

Step 9: Calculate *sum of squares between* (b) *groups* (SSb):

(t) − (r) = _____ (u)   (t) − (r) = _____ (u)

Step 10: Calculate *sum of squares within* (w) *groups* (SSw):

(s) − (u) = _____ (v)   (s) − (u) = _____ (v)

Step 11: Calculate degrees of freedom (d.f.):

d.f. for SSt: (q) − 1 = _____

d.f. for SSb: *n* treatments − 1 = _____

d.f. for SSw: (d.f. for SSt) − (d.f. for SSb) = _____

Step 12: The mean squares (MS) are then calculated as sum of squares divided by the d.f.

$$\text{MSb} = \frac{(u)}{\text{d.f. for SSb}} = \underline{\hspace{2cm}}$$

$$\text{MSw} = \frac{(v)}{\text{d.f. for SSw}} = \underline{\hspace{2cm}}$$

Step 13: Calculate test of significance (*F*): $F = \dfrac{\text{MSb}}{\text{MSw}} =$

ANOVA RESULTS ARE USUALLY REPRESENTED IN A TABLE

Source of variation	Sum of squares	d.f.	MS	F (calculated)	F-critical value (at 5%)
Total	_____ (s)	_____ d.f. SSt			
Between groups	_____ (u)	_____ d.f. SSb	_____ MSb	_____ (F)	_____
Within groups	_____ (v)	_____ d.f. SSw	_____ MSw		

When reading the table (found at the end of Appendix IX) for the *F*-critical value at 5%, you use the d.f. SSb as the numerator value (the top row) and the d.f. SSw as the denominator value (vertical column). If the calculated *F* value is *greater than* the critical value, then you can conclude that *the treatment means are significantly different from each other.*

If the *F* value is significantly different, then there are *other* tests that can determine which of the treatments are specifically different from each other (some may not be). Those tests are not in this book, but you can find them online. Generally, we suggest you have your students analyze them graphically (as per Chapter 3 or 4).

Check the appropriate box:

Significant ☐   Nonsignificant ☐

Assumptions for this test to be valid:

1. The samples were chosen randomly.

2. The data scatter about the means is more or less the same "width" for each group (similar standard deviations).

3. The data scatter is more close to the means and less away from the means (a "normal" distribution).

4. The data in each group or treatment are *independent* of the other groups (in other words, they're not repeated measures on the same individuals or samples getting a different treatment—there's a special test for that). (Using this test if you have multiple samples from the same individual *underestimates* significant differences found. You can use it, just be aware of this.)

5. The data in each group or treatment are *independent* of the samples *in that group* (in other words, they're not repeated measures on the same individuals or samples *within* a treatment—there's a special test for that). (Using this test if you have multiple samples from the same individual *underestimates* significant differences found. You can use it, just be aware of this.)

WORKED-OUT ANOVA WORKSHEET

(Using the dog data from Table 6.2, p. 42)

	Treatment 1: Poodle		Treatment 2: Labrador		Treatment 3: Schnauzer		Treatment 4: Doberman	
	(a)	(a) × (a)	(b)	(b) × (b)	(c)	(c) × (c)	(d)	(d) × (d)
1	14	196	17	289	10	100	8	64
2	13	169	10	100	8	64	9	81
3	13	169	16	256	9	81	6	36
4	15	225	8	64	11	121	8	64
5	17	289	9	81	9	81	7	49
6								
7								
8								
9								
10								
11								
12								
13								
14								
15								
Sum	72 (c)	1,048 (d)	60 (e)	790 (f)	47 (g)	447(h)	38 (i)	294 (j)
Count	5 (k)		5 (l)		5 (m)		5 (n)	

Step 1: Enter data in rows (a) through (d) (assuming four different treatments or observation categories; more may be added).

Step 2: Square values in each of (a) through (d), and put in column immediately to the right.

Step 3: Sum each column, and put results on Sum row.

Step 4: Count measures in each column (a) through (d), and enter them on the Count row.

Step 5: Calculate full table values:

Total sum: (c) + (e) + (g) + (i) = ___217___ (o)

Total sum of squared numbers: (d) + (f) + (h) + (j) = ___2,579___ (p)

Total Count: (k) + (l) + (m) + (n) = ___20___ (q)

Step 6: Calculate *correction term*: (o) × $\dfrac{(o)}{(q)}$ = _2,354.45_ (r)

Step 7: Calculate *sum of squares total* (SSt): (p) − (r) = _224.55_ (s)

Step 8: Calculate: $\dfrac{(c) \times (c)}{(k)}$ + $\dfrac{(e) \times (e)}{(l)}$ + $\dfrac{(g) \times (g)}{(m)}$ + $\dfrac{(i) \times (i)}{(n)}$ = _2,487.4_ (t)

Step 9: Calculate *sum of squares between* (b) *groups* (SSb):

(t) − (r) = _132.95_ (u)

Step 10: Calculate *sum of squares within* (w) *groups* (SSw):

Step 11: Calculate degrees of freedom (d.f.):

d.f. for SSt: (q) − 1 = _19_

d.f. for SSb: number of treatments − 1 = _3_

d.f. for SSw: (d.f. for SSt) − (d.f. for SSb) = _16_

Step 12: The mean squares (MS) are then calculated as sum of squares divided by the d.f.

MSb = $\dfrac{(u)}{\text{d.f. for SSb}}$ = _44.3167_

MSw = $\dfrac{(v)}{\text{d.f. for SSw}}$ = _5.725_

Step 13: Calculate test of significance (*F*): $F = \dfrac{\text{MSb}}{\text{MSw}}$ = _7.74_

ANOVA RESULTS ARE USUALLY REPRESENTED IN A TABLE

Source of variation	Sum of squares	d.f.	MS	F (calculated)	F-critical value (at 5%)
Total	_224.55_ (s)	_19_ d.f. SSt			
Between groups	_132.95_ (u)	_3_ d.f. SSb	_44.317_ MSb	7.74	_3.2_
Within groups	_91.6_ (v)	_16_ d.f. SSw	_5.725_ MSw		

When reading the table (found at the end of Appendix IX) for the *F*-critical value at 5%, you use the d.f. SSb as the numerator value (the top row) and the d.f. SSw as the denominator value (vertical column). If the calculated *F* value is *greater than* the critical value, then you can conclude that *the treatment means are significantly different from each other*.

If the *F* value is significantly different, then there are *other* tests that can determine which of the treatments are specifically different from each other (some may not be). Those tests are not in this book, but you can find them online. Generally, we suggest you have your students analyze them graphically (as per Chapter 3 or 4).

Check the appropriate box:

Significant ☒   Nonsignificant ☐

FIGURE A9.1

Time for different dog breeds to run 30 m

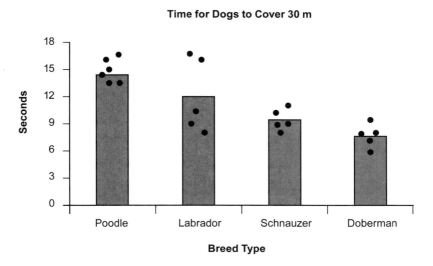

By examining the raw data and looking at the overlap in the data scatter, you could make some inferences now that you know there are statistically significant differences in the times. The schnauzer and Doberman speeds are probably not significantly different, whereas both are probably significantly faster than the poodle. The variations in Labrador times are so great that they are probably not significantly different from either the poodle, the schnauzer, or the Doberman.

REGRESSION ANALYSIS AND CORRELATION COEFFICIENTS WORKSHEET

	Treatment 1: _____	Treatment 2: _____			
	(X)	(Y)	(X) × (X)	(Y) × (Y)	(X) × (Y)
1					
2					
3					
4					
5					
6					
7					
8					
9					
10					
11					
12					
13					
14					
15					
Sum	(a)	(b)	(c)	(d)	(e)
Count	(f)				

Step 1: Calculate product for each pair for (X) × (X), (Y) × (Y), and (X) × (Y), and enter them in table.

Step 2: Calculate sum for each column and put results on Sum row. Count number of pairs of data and enter at (f).

Step 3: (e) × (f) = _____ (g)

Step 4: (c) × (f) = _____ (h)

Step 5: (d) × (f) = _____ (i)

Step 6: (a) × (a) = _____ (j)

Step 7: (b) × (b) = _____ (k)

Step 8: (a) × (b) = _____ (l)

Step 9: (g) – (l) = _____ (m)

Step 10: (h) – (j) = _____ (n)

Step 11: (i) – (k) = _____ (o)

Step 12: (n) × (o) = _____ (p)

Step 13: $\sqrt{(p)}$ = _____ (q)

Step 14: $r = \dfrac{(m)}{(q)}$ = _____ (sign is important as it denotes slope: positive rises from the left)

   The r-squared (× 100) is the percentage of variation in variable Y explained by the

   variable X. The closer it is to 1, the closer the data points are to the line on average.

Step 15: r-squared = $r × r$ = _____

CALCULATING THE LINE OF BEST FIT

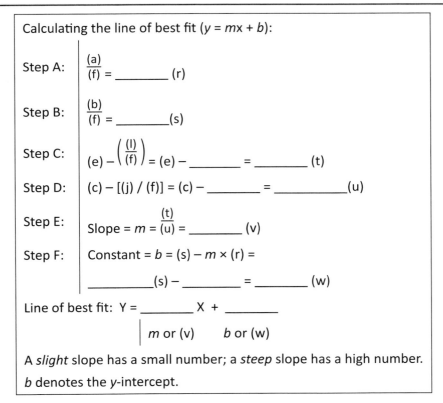

Calculating the line of best fit ($y = m$x + b):

Step A: $\dfrac{(a)}{(f)}$ = _____ (r)

Step B: $\dfrac{(b)}{(f)}$ = _____ (s)

Step C: $(e) - \left(\dfrac{(l)}{(f)} \right)$ = (e) – _____ = _____ (t)

Step D: (c) – [(j) / (f)] = (c) – _____ = _____(u)

Step E: Slope = m = $\dfrac{(t)}{(u)}$ = _____ (v)

Step F: Constant = b = (s) – m × (r) =

   _____(s) – _____ = _____ (w)

Line of best fit: Y = _____ X + _____

       m or (v) b or (w)

A *slight* slope has a small number; a *steep* slope has a high number.

b denotes the *y*-intercept.

WORKED-OUT REGRESSION ANALYSIS AND CORRELATION COEFFICIENT WORKSHEET

(Using the arm- and leg-length data from Table 6.7, p. 44)

	Treatment 1: Arm length	Treatment 2: Leg length			
	(X)	(Y)	(X) × (X)	(Y) × (Y)	(X) × (Y)
1	60.5	67.7	3,660.25	4,583.29	4,095.85
2	63.5	70.3	4,032.25	4,942.09	4,464.05
3	63.6	69.6	4,044.96	4,844.16	4,426.56
4	68.3	75.7	4,664.89	5,730.49	5,170.31
5	69.8	78.1	4,872.04	6,099.61	5,451.38
6	73.4	81.3	5,387.56	6,609.69	5,967.42
7	74.8	83.3	5,595.04	6,938.89	6,230.84
8	76.1	84.7	5,791.21	7,174.09	6,445.67
9	76.3	84.5	5,821.69	7,140.25	6,447.35
10	78.4	86.8	6,146.56	7,534.24	6,805.12
11	79.3	86.8	6,288.49	7,534.24	6,883.24
12	80.2	88.8	6,432.04	7,885.44	7,121.76
13	82.3	91.6	6,773.29	8,390.56	7,538.68
14	83.1	93.0	6,905.61	8,649.00	7,728.30
15	87.2	95.4	7,603.84	9,101.16	8,318.88
Sum	1,116.8 (a)	1,237.6 (b)	8,4019.72 (c)	103,157.2 (d)	93,095.41 (e)
Count	15 (f)				

Step 1: Calculate product for each pair for (X) × (X), (Y) × (Y), and (X) × (Y), and enter them in table.

Step 2: Calculate sum for each column and put results on Sum row. Count number of pairs of data and enter at (f).

Step 3: (e) × (f) = _1,396,431_ (g)

Step 4: (c) × (f) = _1,260,295_ (h)

Step 5: (d) × (f) = _1,547,358_ (i)

Step 6: (a) × (a) = _1,247,242_ (j)

Step 7: (b) × (b) = _1,531,653_ (k)

Step 8: (a) × (b) = _1,382,151_ (l)

Step 9: (g) – (l) = _14,279.47_ (m)

Step 10: (h) – (j) = _13,053.56_ (n)

Step 11: (i) – (k) = _15,704.24_ (o)

Step 12: (n) × (o) = _204,996,239_ (p)

Step 13: $\sqrt{(p)}$ = _14,317.69_ (q)

Step 14: $r = \dfrac{(m)}{(q)}$ = _+0.997330594_ (sign is important as it denotes slope: positive rises from the left)

The r-squared (× 100) is the percentage of variation in variable Y explained by the variable X. The closer it is to 1, the closer the data points are to the line on average.

Step 15: r-squared = $r \times r$ = _0.9946683_

CALCULATING THE LINE OF BEST FIT

Calculating the line of best fit ($y = mx + b$):

Step A: $\dfrac{(a)}{(f)}$ = _74.453_ (r)

Step B: $\dfrac{(b)}{(f)}$ = _82.506_ (s)

Step C: $(e) - \left(\dfrac{(l)}{(f)}\right)$ = (e) – _92,143_ = _951.965_ (t)

Step D: (c) – [(j) / (f)] = (c) – _83,149_ = _870.237_ (u)

Step E: Slope = $m = \dfrac{(t)}{(u)}$ = _1.09391_ (v)

Step F: Constant = b = (s) – m × (r) =

_82.506_ (s) – _81.445_ = _1.062_ (w)

Line of best fit: Y = _1.0939_ X + _1.062_

A *slight* slope has a small number; a *steep* slope has a high number.

b denotes the *y*-intercept.

F-TABLE CRITICAL VALUES

Calculated values above these indicate 5% significantly different means.

d.f. of SSb

d.f. of SSw	1	2	3	4	5	6	7	8	9	10	11	12	13	14	15	16	17	18	19	20
1	161.4	199.5	215.7	224.5	230.1	233.9	236.7	238.9	240.5	241.9	242.9	243.9	244.6	245.3	245.9	246.5	246.9	247.3	247.7	248.0
2	18.51	19.00	19.16	19.25	19.30	19.33	19.35	19.37	19.39	19.40	19.41	19.41	19.42	19.42	19.43	19.43	19.44	19.44	19.44	19.45
3	10.13	9.55	9.28	9.12	9.01	8.94	8.89	8.85	8.81	8.79	8.76	8.75	8.73	8.72	8.70	8.69	8.68	8.68	8.67	8.66
4	7.71	6.94	6.59	6.39	6.26	6.16	6.09	6.04	6.00	5.96	5.94	5.91	5.89	5.87	5.86	5.84	5.83	5.82	5.81	5.80
5	6.61	5.79	5.41	5.19	5.05	4.95	4.88	4.82	4.77	4.74	4.70	4.68	4.66	4.64	4.62	4.60	4.59	4.58	4.57	4.56
6	5.99	5.14	4.76	4.53	4.39	4.28	4.21	4.15	4.10	4.06	4.03	4.00	3.98	3.96	3.94	3.92	3.91	3.90	3.88	3.87
7	5.59	4.74	4.35	4.12	3.97	3.87	3.79	3.73	3.68	3.64	3.60	3.58	3.55	3.53	3.51	3.49	3.48	3.47	3.46	3.45
8	5.32	4.46	4.07	3.84	3.69	3.58	3.50	3.44	3.39	3.35	3.31	3.28	3.26	3.24	3.22	3.20	3.19	3.17	3.16	3.15
9	5.12	4.26	3.86	3.63	3.48	3.37	3.29	3.23	3.18	3.14	3.10	3.07	3.05	3.03	3.01	2.99	2.97	2.96	2.95	2.94
10	4.97	4.10	3.71	3.48	3.33	3.22	3.14	3.07	3.02	2.98	2.94	2.91	2.89	2.87	2.85	2.83	2.81	2.80	2.79	2.77
11	4.84	3.98	3.59	3.36	3.20	3.10	3.01	2.95	2.90	2.85	2.82	2.79	2.76	2.74	2.72	2.70	2.69	2.67	2.66	2.65
12	4.75	3.89	3.49	3.26	3.11	3.00	2.91	2.85	2.80	2.75	2.72	2.69	2.66	2.64	2.62	2.60	2.58	2.57	2.56	2.54
13	4.67	3.81	3.41	3.18	3.03	2.92	2.83	2.77	2.71	2.67	2.64	2.60	2.58	2.55	2.53	2.52	2.50	2.48	2.47	2.46
14	4.60	3.74	3.34	3.11	2.96	2.85	2.76	2.70	2.65	2.60	2.57	2.53	2.51	2.48	2.46	2.45	2.43	2.41	2.40	2.39
15	4.54	3.68	3.29	3.06	2.90	2.79	2.71	2.64	2.59	2.54	2.51	2.48	2.45	2.42	2.40	2.39	2.37	2.35	2.34	2.33
16	4.49	3.63	3.24	3.01	2.85	2.74	2.66	2.59	2.54	2.49	2.46	2.43	2.40	2.37	2.35	2.33	2.32	2.30	2.29	2.28
17	4.45	3.59	3.20	2.97	2.81	2.70	2.61	2.55	2.49	2.45	2.41	2.38	2.35	2.33	2.31	2.29	2.27	2.26	2.24	2.23
18	4.41	3.56	3.16	2.93	2.77	2.66	2.58	2.51	2.46	2.41	2.37	2.34	2.31	2.29	2.27	2.25	2.23	2.22	2.20	2.19
19	4.38	3.52	3.13	2.90	2.74	2.63	2.54	2.48	2.42	2.38	2.34	2.31	2.28	2.26	2.23	2.22	2.20	2.18	2.17	2.16
20	4.35	3.49	3.10	2.87	2.71	2.60	2.51	2.45	2.39	2.35	2.31	2.28	2.25	2.23	2.20	2.18	2.17	2.15	2.14	2.12
21	4.33	3.47	3.07	2.84	2.69	2.57	2.49	2.42	2.37	2.32	2.28	2.25	2.22	2.20	2.18	2.16	2.14	2.12	2.11	2.10
22	4.30	3.44	3.05	2.82	2.66	2.55	2.46	2.40	2.34	2.30	2.26	2.23	2.20	2.17	2.15	2.13	2.11	2.10	2.08	2.07
23	4.28	3.42	3.03	2.80	2.64	2.53	2.44	2.38	2.32	2.28	2.24	2.20	2.18	2.15	2.13	2.11	2.09	2.08	2.06	2.05
24	4.26	3.40	3.01	2.78	2.62	2.51	2.42	2.36	2.30	2.26	2.22	2.18	2.16	2.13	2.11	2.09	2.07	2.05	2.04	2.03
25	4.24	3.39	2.99	2.76	2.60	2.49	2.41	2.34	2.28	2.24	2.20	2.17	2.14	2.11	2.09	2.07	2.05	2.04	2.02	2.01
26	4.23	3.37	2.98	2.74	2.59	2.47	2.39	2.32	2.27	2.22	2.18	2.15	2.12	2.09	2.07	2.05	2.03	2.02	2.00	1.99

NATIONAL SCIENCE TEACHERS ASSOCIATION

d.f. of SSw									d.f. of SSb											
	1	2	3	4	5	6	7	8	9	10	11	12	13	14	15	16	17	18	19	20
27	4.21	3.35	2.96	2.73	2.57	2.46	2.37	2.31	2.25	2.20	2.17	2.13	2.10	2.08	2.06	2.04	2.02	2.00	1.99	1.97
28	4.20	3.34	2.95	2.71	2.56	2.45	2.36	2.29	2.24	2.19	2.15	2.12	2.09	2.06	2.04	2.02	2.00	1.99	1.97	1.96
29	4.18	3.33	2.93	2.70	2.55	2.43	2.35	2.28	2.22	2.18	2.14	2.10	2.08	2.05	2.03	2.01	1.99	1.97	1.96	1.95
30	4.17	3.32	2.92	2.69	2.53	2.42	2.33	2.27	2.21	2.17	2.13	2.09	2.06	2.04	2.02	2.00	1.98	1.96	1.95	1.93
31	4.16	3.31	2.91	2.68	2.52	2.41	2.32	2.26	2.20	2.15	2.11	2.08	2.05	2.03	2.00	1.98	1.97	1.95	1.93	1.92
32	4.15	3.30	2.90	2.67	2.51	2.40	2.31	2.24	2.19	2.14	2.10	2.07	2.04	2.02	1.99	1.97	1.95	1.94	1.92	1.91
33	4.14	3.29	2.89	2.66	2.50	2.39	2.30	2.24	2.18	2.13	2.09	2.06	2.03	2.00	1.98	1.96	1.94	1.93	1.91	1.90
34	4.13	3.28	2.88	2.65	2.49	2.38	2.29	2.23	2.17	2.12	2.08	2.05	2.02	2.00	1.97	1.95	1.93	1.92	1.90	1.89
35	4.12	3.27	2.87	2.64	2.49	2.37	2.29	2.22	2.16	2.11	2.08	2.04	2.01	1.99	1.96	1.94	1.92	1.91	1.89	1.88
36	4.11	3.26	2.87	2.63	2.48	2.36	2.28	2.21	2.15	2.11	2.07	2.03	2.00	1.98	1.95	1.93	1.92	1.90	1.88	1.87
37	4.11	3.25	2.86	2.63	2.47	2.36	2.27	2.20	2.15	2.10	2.06	2.03	2.00	1.97	1.95	1.93	1.91	1.90	1.88	1.86
38	4.10	3.25	2.85	2.62	2.46	2.35	2.26	2.19	2.14	2.09	2.05	2.02	1.99	1.96	1.94	1.92	1.90	1.88	1.87	1.85
39	4.09	3.24	2.85	2.61	2.46	2.34	2.26	2.19	2.13	2.08	2.04	2.01	1.98	1.95	1.93	1.91	1.89	1.88	1.86	1.85
40	4.09	3.23	2.84	2.61	2.45	2.34	2.25	2.18	2.12	2.08	2.04	2.00	1.97	1.95	1.92	1.90	1.89	1.88	1.85	1.84
41	4.08	3.23	2.83	2.60	2.44	2.33	2.24	2.17	2.12	2.07	2.03	2.00	1.97	1.94	1.92	1.90	1.88	1.87	1.85	1.83
42	4.07	3.22	2.83	2.59	2.44	2.32	2.24	2.17	2.11	2.07	2.03	1.99	1.96	1.94	1.91	1.89	1.87	1.86	1.84	1.83
43	4.07	3.21	2.82	2.59	2.43	2.32	2.23	2.16	2.11	2.06	2.02	1.99	1.96	1.93	1.91	1.89	1.87	1.85	1.83	1.82
44	4.06	3.21	2.82	2.58	2.43	2.31	2.23	2.16	2.10	2.05	2.01	1.98	1.95	1.92	1.90	1.88	1.86	1.84	1.83	1.81
45	4.06	3.20	2.81	2.58	2.42	2.31	2.22	2.15	2.10	2.05	2.01	1.97	1.95	1.92	1.90	1.87	1.86	1.84	1.82	1.81
46	4.05	3.20	2.81	2.57	2.42	2.30	2.22	2.15	2.09	2.04	2.00	1.97	1.94	1.91	1.89	1.87	1.85	1.83	1.82	1.80
47	4.05	3.20	2.80	2.57	2.41	2.30	2.21	2.14	2.09	2.04	2.00	1.97	1.94	1.91	1.89	1.86	1.85	1.83	1.81	1.80
48	4.04	3.19	2.80	2.57	2.41	2.30	2.21	2.14	2.08	2.04	2.00	1.96	1.93	1.90	1.88	1.86	1.84	1.82	1.81	1.79
49	4.04	3.19	2.79	2.56	2.40	2.29	2.20	2.13	2.08	2.03	1.99	1.96	1.93	1.90	1.88	1.86	1.84	1.82	1.80	1.79
50	4.03	3.18	2.79	2.56	2.40	2.29	2.20	2.13	2.07	2.03	1.99	1.95	1.92	1.90	1.87	1.85	1.83	1.81	1.80	1.78
51	4.03	3.18	2.79	2.55	2.40	2.28	2.20	2.13	2.07	2.02	1.98	1.95	1.92	1.89	1.87	1.85	1.83	1.81	1.80	1.78
52	4.03	3.18	2.78	2.55	2.39	2.28	2.19	2.12	2.07	2.02	1.98	1.94	1.91	1.89	1.86	1.84	1.82	1.81	1.79	1.78
53	4.02	3.17	2.78	2.55	2.39	2.28	2.19	2.12	2.06	2.02	1.98	1.94	1.91	1.88	1.86	1.84	1.82	1.80	1.79	1.77

d.f. of SSw	1	2	3	4	5	6	7	8	9	10	11	12	13	14	15	16	17	18	19	20
54	4.02	3.17	2.78	2.54	2.39	2.27	2.19	2.12	2.06	2.01	1.97	1.94	1.91	1.88	1.86	1.84	1.82	1.80	1.78	1.77
55	4.02	3.17	2.77	2.54	2.38	2.27	2.18	2.11	2.06	2.01	1.97	1.93	1.90	1.88	1.85	1.83	1.81	1.80	1.78	1.76
56	4.01	3.16	2.77	2.54	2.38	2.27	2.18	2.11	2.05	2.01	1.96	1.93	1.90	1.87	1.85	1.83	1.81	1.79	1.78	1.76
57	4.01	3.16	2.77	2.53	2.38	2.26	2.18	2.11	2.05	2.00	1.96	1.93	1.90	1.87	1.85	1.82	1.81	1.79	1.77	1.76
58	4.01	3.16	2.76	2.53	2.37	2.26	2.17	2.10	2.05	2.00	1.96	1.92	1.89	1.87	1.84	1.82	1.80	1.79	1.77	1.75
59	4.00	3.15	2.76	2.53	2.37	2.26	2.17	2.10	2.04	2.00	1.96	1.92	1.89	1.86	1.84	1.82	1.80	1.78	1.77	1.75
60	4.00	3.15	2.76	2.53	2.37	2.25	2.17	2.10	2.04	1.99	1.95	1.92	1.89	1.86	1.84	1.82	1.80	1.78	1.76	1.75
61	4.00	3.15	2.76	2.52	2.37	2.25	2.16	2.09	2.04	1.99	1.95	1.92	1.88	1.86	1.83	1.81	1.79	1.78	1.76	1.75
62	4.00	3.15	2.75	2.52	2.36	2.25	2.16	2.09	2.04	1.99	1.95	1.91	1.88	1.86	1.83	1.81	1.79	1.77	1.76	1.74
63	3.99	3.14	2.75	2.52	2.36	2.25	2.16	2.09	2.03	1.99	1.94	1.91	1.88	1.86	1.83	1.81	1.79	1.77	1.75	1.74
64	3.99	3.14	2.75	2.52	2.36	2.24	2.16	2.09	2.03	1.98	1.94	1.91	1.88	1.85	1.83	1.80	1.79	1.77	1.75	1.74
65	3.99	3.14	2.75	2.51	2.36	2.24	2.15	2.08	2.03	1.98	1.94	1.90	1.87	1.85	1.82	1.80	1.78	1.77	1.75	1.73
66	3.99	3.14	2.74	2.51	2.35	2.24	2.15	2.08	2.03	1.98	1.94	1.90	1.87	1.85	1.82	1.80	1.78	1.76	1.74	1.73
67	3.98	3.13	2.74	2.51	2.35	2.24	2.15	2.08	2.02	1.98	1.94	1.90	1.87	1.85	1.82	1.80	1.78	1.77	1.74	1.73
68	3.98	3.13	2.74	2.51	2.35	2.24	2.15	2.08	2.02	1.97	1.93	1.90	1.87	1.84	1.82	1.80	1.78	1.77	1.74	1.73
69	3.98	3.13	2.74	2.51	2.35	2.23	2.15	2.08	2.02	1.97	1.93	1.90	1.86	1.84	1.81	1.79	1.77	1.76	1.74	1.73
70	3.98	3.13	2.74	2.50	2.35	2.23	2.14	2.07	2.02	1.97	1.93	1.89	1.86	1.84	1.81	1.79	1.77	1.75	1.74	1.72
71	3.98	3.13	2.73	2.50	2.34	2.23	2.14	2.07	2.02	1.97	1.93	1.89	1.86	1.83	1.81	1.79	1.77	1.75	1.74	1.72
72	3.97	3.12	2.73	2.50	2.34	2.23	2.14	2.07	2.01	1.97	1.92	1.89	1.86	1.83	1.81	1.79	1.77	1.75	1.73	1.72
73	3.97	3.12	2.73	2.50	2.34	2.23	2.14	2.07	2.01	1.96	1.92	1.89	1.86	1.83	1.81	1.78	1.77	1.75	1.73	1.72
74	3.97	3.12	2.73	2.50	2.34	2.22	2.14	2.07	2.01	1.96	1.92	1.89	1.86	1.83	1.80	1.78	1.76	1.75	1.73	1.72
75	3.97	3.12	2.73	2.49	2.34	2.22	2.13	2.06	2.01	1.96	1.92	1.88	1.85	1.83	1.80	1.78	1.76	1.75	1.73	1.71
76	3.97	3.12	2.73	2.49	2.34	2.22	2.13	2.06	2.01	1.96	1.92	1.88	1.85	1.82	1.80	1.78	1.76	1.74	1.73	1.71
77	3.97	3.12	2.72	2.49	2.33	2.22	2.13	2.06	2.01	1.96	1.92	1.88	1.85	1.82	1.80	1.78	1.76	1.74	1.72	1.71
78	3.96	3.11	2.72	2.49	2.33	2.22	2.13	2.06	2.00	1.95	1.91	1.88	1.85	1.82	1.80	1.78	1.76	1.74	1.72	1.71
79	3.96	3.11	2.72	2.49	2.33	2.22	2.13	2.06	2.00	1.95	1.91	1.88	1.85	1.82	1.80	1.77	1.75	1.74	1.72	1.71

d.f. of SSb

d.f. of SSw	1	2	3	4	5	6	7	8	9	10	11	12	13	14	15	16	17	18	19	20
																			d.f. of SSb	
80	3.96	3.11	2.72	2.49	2.33	2.21	2.13	2.06	2.00	1.95	1.91	1.88	1.85	1.82	1.79	1.77	1.75	1.73	1.72	1.70
81	3.96	3.11	2.72	2.48	2.33	2.21	2.13	2.06	2.00	1.95	1.91	1.87	1.84	1.82	1.79	1.77	1.75	1.73	1.72	1.70
82	3.96	3.11	2.72	2.48	2.33	2.21	2.12	2.05	2.00	1.95	1.91	1.87	1.84	1.81	1.79	1.77	1.75	1.73	1.72	1.70
83	3.96	3.11	2.72	2.48	2.32	2.21	2.12	2.05	2.00	1.95	1.91	1.87	1.84	1.81	1.79	1.77	1.75	1.73	1.71	1.70
84	3.96	3.11	2.71	2.48	2.32	2.21	2.12	2.05	1.99	1.95	1.91	1.87	1.84	1.81	1.79	1.77	1.75	1.73	1.71	1.70
85	3.95	3.10	2.71	2.48	2.32	2.21	2.12	2.05	1.99	1.94	1.90	1.87	1.84	1.81	1.79	1.76	1.74	1.73	1.71	1.69
86	3.95	3.10	2.71	2.48	2.32	2.21	2.12	2.05	1.99	1.94	1.90	1.87	1.84	1.81	1.78	1.76	1.74	1.73	1.71	1.69
87	3.95	3.10	2.71	2.48	2.32	2.21	2.12	2.05	1.99	1.94	1.90	1.87	1.83	1.81	1.78	1.76	1.74	1.72	1.71	1.69
88	3.95	3.10	2.71	2.48	2.32	2.20	2.12	2.05	1.99	1.94	1.90	1.86	1.83	1.81	1.78	1.76	1.74	1.72	1.71	1.69
89	3.95	3.10	2.71	2.47	2.32	2.20	2.11	2.04	1.99	1.94	1.90	1.86	1.83	1.80	1.78	1.76	1.74	1.72	1.71	1.69
90	3.95	3.10	2.71	2.47	2.32	2.20	2.11	2.04	1.99	1.94	1.90	1.86	1.83	1.80	1.78	1.76	1.74	1.72	1.70	1.69
91	3.95	3.10	2.71	2.47	2.32	2.20	2.11	2.04	1.98	1.94	1.90	1.86	1.83	1.80	1.78	1.76	1.74	1.72	1.70	1.69
92	3.95	3.10	2.70	2.47	2.31	2.20	2.11	2.04	1.98	1.94	1.89	1.86	1.83	1.80	1.78	1.76	1.74	1.72	1.70	1.69
93	3.94	3.09	2.70	2.47	2.31	2.20	2.11	2.04	1.98	1.93	1.89	1.86	1.83	1.80	1.78	1.75	1.73	1.72	1.70	1.68
94	3.94	3.09	2.70	2.47	2.31	2.20	2.11	2.04	1.98	1.93	1.89	1.86	1.83	1.80	1.77	1.75	1.73	1.72	1.70	1.68
95	3.94	3.09	2.70	2.47	2.31	2.20	2.11	2.04	1.98	1.93	1.89	1.86	1.82	1.80	1.77	1.75	1.73	1.71	1.70	1.68
96	3.94	3.09	2.70	2.47	2.31	2.19	2.11	2.04	1.98	1.93	1.89	1.85	1.82	1.80	1.77	1.75	1.73	1.71	1.70	1.68
97	3.94	3.09	2.70	2.47	2.31	2.19	2.11	2.04	1.98	1.93	1.89	1.85	1.82	1.80	1.77	1.75	1.73	1.71	1.70	1.68
98	3.94	3.09	2.70	2.47	2.31	2.19	2.10	2.03	1.98	1.93	1.89	1.85	1.82	1.79	1.77	1.75	1.73	1.71	1.69	1.68
99	3.94	3.09	2.70	2.46	2.31	2.19	2.10	2.03	1.98	1.93	1.89	1.85	1.82	1.79	1.77	1.75	1.73	1.71	1.69	1.68
100	3.94	3.09	2.70	2.46	2.31	2.19	2.10	2.03	1.98	1.93	1.89	1.85	1.82	1.79	1.77	1.75	1.73	1.71	1.69	1.68

RESOURCES

Alreck, P. L., and R. B. Settle. 1985. *The survey research handbook.* Homewood, IL: Irwin, Inc.

Bruning, J. L., and B. L. Kintz. 1978. *Computational handbook of statistics.* Glenview, IL: Scott Foresman and Company.

Clement, J. J., and M. A. Rea-Ramiriz, eds. 2008. *Model based learning and instruction in science.* New York: Springer.

Collins, H. 2010. *Tacit and explicit knowledge.* Chicago: University of Chicago Press.

Gross, A. G. 1996. *The rhetoric of science.* Cambridge, MA: Harvard University Press.

Huff, D. 1982. *How to lie with statistics.* New York: W. W. Norton and Company.

Jones, G. E. 1995. *How to lie with charts.* San Francisco: Sybex.

Kingsland, S. E. 1995. *Modeling nature: Episodes in the history of population ecology.* 2nd ed. Chicago: The University of Chicago Press.

Koosis, D. 1985. *Statistics: A self-teaching guide.* 3rd ed. New York: John Wiley and Sons.

Kosslyn, S. M. 1994. *Elements of graph design.* New York: W. H. Freeman and Company.

Laszlo, P. 2006. *Communicating science: A practical guide.* New York: Springer.

Latour, B. 1987. *Science in action: How to follow scientists and engineers through society.* Cambridge, MA: Harvard University Press.

Lefferts, R. 1981. *Elements of graphics: How to prepare charts and graphs for effective reports.* New York: Harper and Row.

Lenoir, T., ed. 1998. *Inscribing science: Scientific texts and the materiality of communication.* Stanford, CA: Stanford University Press.

Lynch, M., and S. Woolgar, eds. 1988. *Representation in scientific practice.* Cambridge, MA: MIT Press.

Norman, G. R., and D. L. Streiner. 1986. *PDQ statistics.* Toronto, Ontario: B.C. Decker, Inc.

Roth, W. M. 1995. *Authentic school science: Knowing and learning in open-inquiry science laboratories.* Boston: Kluwer Academic Publishers.

Roth, W. M. 2003. *Toward an anthropology of graphing: Semiotic and activity-theory perspectives.* Boston: Kluwer Academic Publishers.

Stocklmayer, S. M., M. M. Gore, and C. Bryant, eds. 2001. *Science communication in theory and practice.* Boston: Kluwer Academic Publishers.

Watson, J. M. 2006. *Statistical literacy at schools: Growth and goals.* Mahwah, NJ: Lawrence Erlbaum Associates.

INDEX